Contents

Introduction 5

Chapter **1** What Makes a Successful Salesperson?............ 7

Chapter **2** Selling More by Understanding

Customers 21

Chapter **3** Selling Face-to-Face 39

Chapter **4** Words That Sell 57

Chapter **5** Selling at Events, Trade Fairs and

Exhibitions... 73

Chapter **6** Simple Ways to Boost Sales................................. 83

Chapter **7** Setting the Right Price for Profitable

Sales...97

Chapter **8** Great Customer Service Boost Sales 107

Help List 121

Book List 123

SALES AND SELLING

The Essential Guide

Moi Ali

Sales and Selling: The Essential Guide is also available in accessible formats for people with any degree of visual impairment. The large print edition and e-book (with accessibility features enabled) are available from Need2Know. Please let us know if there are any special features you require and we will do our best to accommodate your needs.

First published in Great Britain in 2012 by
Need2Know
Remus House
Coltsfoot Drive
Peterborough
PE2 9BF
Telephone 01733 898103
Fax 01733 313524
www.need2knowbooks.co.uk

Introduction

Are you self-employed or do you work for a small business? Perhaps you have to sell as part of your role, but you lack the skills or confidence to do it as well as you'd like. Or you feel that you could sharpen up your sales approach, if only you could pick up a few tips and tricks. Maybe you're completely new to sales and don't know how or where to begin. Great! This book is for you.

Without sales, no business can survive. Whatever you sell – goods, services, even yourself and your knowledge and expertise – you need to know how to approach sales. What motivates people to buy? What are the characteristics of successful salespeople? Why might a company place an order with you rather than with one of your competitors? How can you use simple techniques to boost your sales success? Find the answers to these and many other key questions in this practical book.

Salespeople sometimes have a bad reputation for being pushy, aggressive and dishonest. We think of the travelling salesman with his foot wedged in the front door; the con-artist used-car salesman willing to say anything, however untrue, in order to palm off an unreliable vehicle on an unsuspecting purchaser; or the telesales people who cold-call night after night, always just as you are about to relax over a glass of wine and a TV dinner, who simply won't take no for an answer.

The likes of these have given sales a bad name, but there's absolutely no need to feel ashamed about your sales role. Successful salespeople negotiate agreements that are beneficial to their company and a good deal for the customer – that fabled win-win. So if you are a bit shy, or you hate the idea of being forced to make a sale that is completely disadvantageous to the customer, it's time to heave a sigh of relief, because sales should not be like that.

You don't need to be brash, arrogant or 'in yer face' – in fact, it helps if you're not! Nor need you be dishonest, manipulative or scheming. No, you simply have to be an honest broker who is pleasant and personable, with a good product or service, in-depth industry knowledge and a genuine commitment to top-class customer service and to building lasting relationships. If that sounds like you, perfect! We're going to get along well.

This book will help you work out your sales persona so that you're comfortable making pitches using your own unique style. You'll also pick up tips on how to write powerful sales materials – formal sales proposals, mailshots and other marketing and publicity material designed to sell – and you'll learn a bit about the psychology of buying and selling (and its practical application). There's advice on establishing a good rapport with prospective customers and top tips on effective ways for dealing with objections. Action points at the end of each chapter mean that you can improve your sales skills as you progress through the book. By the end, there'll be no holding you back as you move from one successful sale to the next, with ever-growing confidence and an ever-growing contacts book.

Chapter One

What Makes a Successful Salesperson?

Here's a test. A man goes into a shop, asks to see a DellBoy 105E laptop computer, which he then purchases. What has the store owner just sold? A laptop? No, the owner has sold nothing; she has merely served the customer. The customer has bought a laptop. Buying and selling are two different things.

OK, let's replay that scene. The man asks to see the 105E laptop. While he's trying it out, the store owner asks a few questions about usage and needs, and then recommends two further laptop models. She also shows the customer laptop bags, in-car chargers and adjustable laptop stands, as the customer has indicated that he will use the laptop on the move. Having listened carefully to the pros and cons of the various laptops and accessories, and considered his own needs and budget, the customer decides to take the DellBoy 777X laptop, leather carrying case and car charger. Now the shop owner can take some credit for selling something!

Pizza restaurants use this technique all the time. Just think how often you've ordered garlic bread or a side salad that you didn't plan on having, just because the waiter asked you if you wanted any of these with your margarita!

Selling is a proactive process, not a reactive event. Setting out your goods and services and awaiting purchases is too passive. Your business will not grow if you take that tack; in tough economic times, it may even collapse.

So, the first trait of a successful salesperson is that they are proactive. You won't find them sitting on their backsides daydreaming, idly browsing the Internet looking at Facebook, Friends Reunited and other non-work websites, or wasting time chatting by the photocopier or the coffee machine. The successful salesperson is busy seeking out and creating opportunities to make

'The first trait of a successful salesperson is that they are proactive.'

a sale. It is only the lazy and ineffectual who rely on sales coming to them; successful people go out and make their own lucky breaks. Recently at a car boot sale, a woman walked by carrying a bread maker. A nearby stallholder seized the opportunity, calling out: 'Hey gorgeous, want a bread maker recipe book? To you, it's only £1!' and thus he made a successful sale that would not have occurred without his proactive attitude. It's a small-scale example, but it demonstrates well the attributes of a successful salesperson. Using charm, he palmed off an unwanted book and boosted his boot sale takings in the process; she left with a useful clutch of recipes for her newly-purchased second-hand bread maker. Both were happy bunnies.

Does all of that proactivity sound a bit too much like hard work? Better get used to it, because sales will not just land on your lap. You'll have to work at them, and it will be hard – but it will be so worthwhile, and the more you achieve, the more enjoyable it will become. So attribute number two for a successful salesperson is that they are hard-working.

Finding your sales persona

Have you ever been on the receiving end of the attentions of one of those aggressive salespeople, the type that corners customers and pressures or browbeats them into making reluctant purchases? There's no need for you to be like that. In fact, you're far less likely to find success long term if you adopt that approach. Successful salespeople use gentle persuasion, not bullying tactics. They solve customer problems, rather than create them!

Never feel that you must model yourself on that stereotypical salesperson. Find your own style, one suited to your natural personality. Successful sellers can be quiet, calm and self-deprecating. Yes, really! Or they can be outgoing, flamboyant and brimming with confidence. There is no one personality type. We all have to find our own sales style and persona, something that we are comfortable with and that works for us. Take a moment to think about what feels right for you.

However, while we may each adopt a different or unique approach to sales, there are a number of things that successful salespeople share.

Qualities of a successful salesperson

Successful salespeople are:

- Hard-working – They put in the time and do things properly, without cutting corners. They will arrive early, work through lunch or work late in order to secure an order, and although they achieve a healthy work/life balance, they are not clock-watchers.

- Well organised – They are always well prepared for meetings and sales pitches and well organised in the workplace, with tidy desks and up-to-date files.

- Proactive – They don't sit around waiting for sales, or put off making appointments with prospects. They pick up the phone and get on with it.

- Enthusiastic – Work isn't a chore or a bore, it's challenging yet fun and they effortlessly communicate their enthusiasm for it.

- Good time managers – They make the most of the working day, planning calls and appointments to maximise their time and effectiveness.

- Knowledgeable – They know their products/services and their market. They research their customers and their competitors.

- Attentive – They are interested in their customers, listen and remember because they recognise the importance of building long-term relationships.

- Confident – About themselves, their company and their products/services. Their quiet confidence instils confidence in potential customers. They recognise the difference between confidence and arrogance.

- Persuasive – They know their products, their customers and their market, and they use that knowledge to devise persuasive pitches and proposals. They know that persuasive and pushy are two different things and that while they must always strive for the former, they must never succumb to the latter.

- Self-challenging – Like other mere mortals, they get scared and nervous, but they push themselves and tackle the fears that may hold some of us back. They are committed to self-improvement and they seek to identify and address any shortcomings in order to improve their personal effectiveness.

Every effective salesperson will embody most of these positive traits, but we display them in different ways because each of us is unique. Think about which of these qualities you possess. Revisit the above list and tick the ones that are your strong points. Celebrate. Pat yourself on the back for having so many good qualities that leave you so well placed to excel in sales.

Of course, no one's perfect. You're bound to have weaknesses. Are there any gaps that you display? Perhaps you are not attentive enough, or you could be better at managing your time. Draw up a list of characteristics that need further work and devise an action plan to help address any weaknesses. You can read more about how to do this later in the chapter.

Characteristics of a poor salesperson

It's worth spending a moment looking at the behaviours that distinguish a poor salesperson from a good one because we can learn much from what not to do. If you recognise any of the following attributes in yourself, address them now! A bad salesperson:

- Procrastinates – They put off making sales calls, booking appointments with prospective clients, replying to enquiries or dealing with complaints. They may look busy, but they tend to do the things that they enjoy rather than the things that make a difference to their sales figures.

- Lives for now – They often try to make (or even force) an immediate one-off sale rather than taking the longer view and looking at the sale as part of a more lasting relationship based on excellent customer service. They live for today and don't think too much about tomorrow.

- Lacks integrity – They may not mind being economical with the truth and some can be downright dishonest and willing to rip people off, so long as they can make a sale that is advantageous to them.

- Demonstrates negativity – They may be so afraid of failure that they set themselves up to fail with their negative attitude. Failure then becomes a self-fulfilling prophesy.

- Shows cockiness – They confuse confidence with arrogance. Their overinflated sense of themselves makes them look vain and foolish and damages their credibility. They may act like they've got the sale 'in the bag' and this will irritate customers and make them less likely to place an order.

- Disrespects – They may secretly harbour contempt for customers, regarding them as suckers or purely as a means to their next bonus.

- Talks too much – Asking lots of questions and listening carefully to the answers is a vital part of the sales process, and salespeople who talk too much fail to pick up important information that could help them secure a sale.

- May be disorganised – Their car, office, desk or files may be in disorder or disarray. They often struggle to lay their hands on the information they need because of their chaotic approach. This may make them late for appointments, which irritates potential buyers. They will forget to follow-up on promises they make. They may be chaotic at home too, and turn up for an important pitch in an unironed outfit and uncombed hair, creating a poor first impression.

Few of us would admit openly to having any of the above negative attributes, but be brutally honest: did any of it sound a bit like you? Take a long, hard look at yourself. Do you display any of these undesirable tendencies? You do? Don't beat yourself up about it, but do make a commitment to tackle it – right now! It's never too late to get organised or to adopt a more positive attitude. Tackle those weaknesses and build on your strengths. Go back and tick anything that applies to you, and we'll look next at how you can do something positive to change things for the better.

Moving out of your comfort zone

When it comes to selling, what kind of a person are you? Are you confident about going out and meeting complete strangers, and happy to get up on your hind legs and make a formal presentation to a group of serious-looking potential buyers? Or do you get rather nervous, panicky even? Inevitably there will be aspects of being a salesperson that you may find daunting or downright difficult. Where do you struggle? Perhaps you are naturally shy and find it hard to make small talk with people. Or you're a bit scatty and find it a strain to keep on top of your paperwork. Whatever your weaknesses, they can be strengthened. You have the ability within you to improve.

Think about what feels natural and comfortable for you when you're selling. Now reflect on whether your natural style is effective. We all have a tendency to operate well within our comfort zone, for the obvious reason: we feel comfortable there! It's safe and familiar. But to succeed, we may need to move out of that warm, happy zone and push ourselves a bit more. This will mean taking on things we feel uncomfortable about doing – making presentations, for example – or tackling our bashfulness.

What do effective salespeople do that you avoid doing? Remind yourself of the characteristics of successful salespeople on page 9. Make a commitment to yourself to start on a course of self-improvement. Tomorrow, do something you would ordinarily avoid, such as making a few cold calls or volunteering to front-up a sales pitch. Better still, why wait until tomorrow. Do it today! Each week tackle another area that is outside your comfort zone, and try to enjoy your new-found skills.

'Whatever your weaknesses, they can be strengthened. You have the ability within you to improve.'

The self-improvement action plan

Draw up a table like the following one, and list all of the things about the sales process that you feel uncomfortable doing. Be clear about why you feel uneasy about these things. Think about how you avoid doing them and reflect on how your avoidance techniques hold you back and prevent you from fulfilling your potential as a top-notch salesperson. Now work out a plan to push at your own boundaries. What action will you commit to take in order to address your shortcomings and set you firmly on the road to being a really successful salesperson?

I feel uncomfortable doing . . . because . . .	I avoid it by . . .	Action
Making presentations . . . Standing up and speaking makes me nervous and self-conscious.	Asking John to do them. John is great at presentations but I lack confidence.	I will attend a course on presentation skills in two weeks' time. I will front the sales presentation scheduled for next month.
Making cold calls . . . I get tongue-tied and don't know how to open the conversation.	Writing or emailing instead . . . I rarely get a reply from the people I write to and feel sure that a personal approach by phone would be more effective.	Tonight I will draft a script on how to open a cold call, and I will practise this aloud until I am fluent. When I get to the office tomorrow I will make five cold calls by 10am.
Making small talk . . . It feels contrived and I'd rather just get on with making a sale.	Getting straight on with the business . . . I suspect that I appear rather cold or aloof with customers when in reality I'm actually quite friendly with people I know.	At Sue's party on Friday night I will make a point of speaking to six people I don't know so that I can practise my small talk.

Winning over wary customers

Salespeople sometimes have a bit of a bad name with the public because a minority of them employ sharp practices. This means that good salespeople – the hard-working, honest ones like you and me – can find ourselves selling to people who may have a negative view of us because they dislike all salespeople following one or two bad past experiences. It is helpful to be aware of this when going to see a potential buyer. Don't take it personally if you encounter a hostile prospect. A successful salesperson recognises that they have to earn trust and respect, never taking it as a given. They're not offended when a customer is initially wary of them or gives them a hard time. If we are to succeed in sales, we need to learn to remain friendly in difficult situations. Our professionalism can often win round a sceptical would-be client. And one thing's for sure: if we meet hostility with hostility, we're never going to charm the prospect and therefore we're never going to make the sale. So remain polite at all times. If nothing else, it's better for your blood pressure!

Breaking the cycle of hostility

'A successful salesperson recognises that they have to earn trust and respect, never taking it as a given.'

Customer has bad experience with salesperson

Next time, customer is hostile towards salesperson

Salesperson responds with hostility

Break the cycle of hostility and restore a customer's faith in salespeople. Most of us find it hard to be unpleasant to someone who is being reasonable and friendly. Set the tone with your professional attitude. Never retaliate; always work to rescue a potentially antagonistic situation with your calm and poise. And remember, most encounters won't be hostile at all, but if you know how to handle things when they are tough, you'll feel more confident. What's more, if an encounter remains hostile, you can always just walk away. It's not the end of the world, and so long as you do it in a calm and polite way, the door may remain open for some future meeting when the prospective client is in a more amenable mood. Successful salespeople never let the fear of a hostile encounter hold them back. Such fears usually fail to materialise and so long as you know how to act, should they arise, there's nothing to fear.

Remaining positive in the face of failure

Not every sales pitch or proposal will result in success. If only! Successful salespeople never let failure knock them back. They regard it as an important part of the sales process, providing an opportunity to take stock and ask some searching questions. What let us down this time? Was the product not good enough and can we improve it? Was the presentation poor and can we rework it? Was it price, our negotiation tactics, or what? Or was it nothing to do with us at all? Perhaps the prospective client didn't place an order with anyone, but was simply seeing what was out there. Maybe next time.

Learn from every failure. Use it as an opportunity to improve your offering, your presentation or some other aspect that may have let you down. If you don't know what caused the customer to go elsewhere, why not ask them. Explain that you were disappointed not to win the business and ask for an indication of why you did not succeed on this occasion. Digest the feedback and then act upon it.

OK, so failure happens. Deal with it positively. Pick yourself up, dust yourself down and set aside any sense of disappointment or feelings of personal rejection, natural though such emotions may be. Focus on future success, not past failure. Never allow failure to hold you back or deter you from giving your all to subsequent sales attempts. Let it make you more determined that your next presentation will be better than the last, with success more likely. Positivity combined with hard work will produce good results. Negative salespeople are rarely successful.

But what if you made a howler of a mistake and that's why you didn't win the business. We're human and we all make mistakes, so stop chastising or punishing yourself for your error. Forgive yourself, put it behind you and move on – but *never* let it happen again!

'Focus on future success, not past failure. Never allow failure to hold you back or deter you from giving your all to subsequent sales attempts.'

Building relationships for future success

A skilled salesperson never regards selling as a series of one-off sales to a succession of different customers. Successful sales careers are built on lasting relationships with valued clients. Sometimes a salesperson will be so determined to make a sale that he or she will push the customer into a reluctant purchase. Or the customer will buy willingly on the strength of the salesperson's promises, but when those promises fail to deliver, the customer becomes disillusioned. Either way, that's a sure-fire way to terminate a relationship before it's even got off the ground.

The illustration below shows how short-sighted it is to ignore long-term relationships. The desperate salesperson uses pushiness or false promises to make a one-off sale. His or her satisfaction with securing the sale is short-lived, because short-termism leads to an endless and thankless task of chasing new customers, made all the harder as word of customer dissatisfaction spreads. After each sale it's back to square 1 to start all over again.

A bad outcome: always back to square 1!

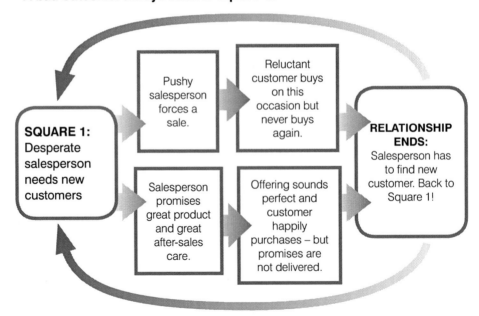

Don't make a sale: build a relationship

Smart salespeople know that in the long run, it's so much easier to build long-term relationships with a small number of loyal clients than it is to constantly find new ones to replace the ones you've lost through your own short-termism. Smart salespeople create happy customers who are happy to buy again and again – and to recommend the company to their friends and colleagues. It's easier to sell to someone who has come to you following a personal recommendation, so it makes sense to invest in those relationships.

A good outcome

Keep on learning and improving

Under no circumstances would a successful salesperson allow themselves to become complacent. People who are accomplished, whether in sales or in any other area of life, never think that they know all there is to know, or that there is no room for improvement. Success involves ongoing self-examination and self-improvement.

Successful salespeople are reflective and thoughtful. They replay recent sales pitches in their head and work out how their performance could be improved. They read books on sales (just like you are now), ever on the lookout for tips and new techniques. They attend talks, presentations and courses on improving sales skills. They review their PowerPoint sales presentations and fine-tune them, and rewrite sales letters to make them more powerful and persuasive. Everything is aimed at being better, being more effective, achieving more. They never allow themselves to stagnate, or to slip into comfortable but ineffective routines or habits, just treading water. No, they keep pushing themselves, trying new ideas, setting higher targets and forging ahead.

Dos and don'ts for sales success

▨ Do reflect on areas for self-improvement – then take action!

▨ Don't ever become complacent or self-satisfied.

▨ Do force yourself to move out of your comfort zone and tackle new things.

▨ Don't ever assume that a sale is 'in the bag' or take a customer for granted.

▨ Do work at building lasting relationships.

▨ Don't avoid things just because they're difficult.

Action points

▨ Look at the section detailing the characteristics of a successful salesperson and think about your own personality. What characteristics do you have that are an attribute to you in your sales role? How can you capitalise on these in your work?

▨ Think about the last time that you were actively sold something (not the last time you bought something!) What did you like about the salesperson's approach? What did you dislike? Is there anything you can learn from the interaction that will influence the way that you will act in the future as a salesperson?

▨ Look up self-improvement resources on the Internet – books, courses and events. Find something that looks useful and buy the book, use the website or attend the course. Start now on the road to self-improvement, whether it's improving your time management or learning how to make perfect presentations.

Summing Up

▨ In this introductory chapter we took an overview of the successful salesperson – what makes a good one and what characterises a bad one.

▨ The focus was on how to move out of your comfort zone to start tackling the things you find difficult, usually the very things that will lead to success.

▨ Self-analysis is important to help you understand what you're good at and where you need to improve.

▨ The emphasis in this chapter was on action – identifying and committing to real things you can do to address any shortcomings and to start to build your skills and confidence.

Chapter Two

Selling More by Understanding Customers

It stands to reason that if you understand why people buy, you'll find it easier to sell to them. Successful salespeople have an insight into their customers, knowing who they are, what motivates them, what their buying behaviour is and what they look for in a service or product. This knowledge and understanding gives the savvy salesperson a competitive advantage, as they already know which buttons to push in order to reach a successful sale. They understand what kind of branding will appeal to their customers, what sort of marketing material will click with them, even where to place adverts in order to reach their target customer. Do you have this level of insight into your customers? No? This chapter will explain how to build up intelligence about your customers to help you sell more successfully – not only to them, but to others like them.

Consumer behaviour and the psychology of spending

Everyone buys for a reason. Even frivolous or unnecessary purchases are motivated by something – if not by need, perhaps by the pure pleasure of ownership. Why do people buy what you are selling? Do you know? A motivation for a fair chunk of our purchases is *need*. We *need* to eat, drink, wash, keep warm, clothed and housed. If you are selling, say, basic foodstuffs, your customers will be buying primarily because food is a necessity for survival: we *need* to eat. Most of us would probably prefer not to have to shell out on expensive gas and electricity, but life without heat and light in our climate simply does not bear thinking about, so we grit our teeth and make the purchase. We'd far rather spend that £1,000 on gadgets and holidays than on a railway season ticket, but travel to work is a necessity so we have no option. It is easier to sell people things they need, for obvious reasons, though even then, a sale is not a dead cert; there will usually be other suppliers who can meet that need and customers, if at all sensible, will want to shop around.

What we *need* changes over time. My mother's generation regarded a washing machine, a vacuum cleaner, a fridge and an indoor toilet as unimaginable luxuries; I regard them as basic necessities, along with a microwave oven, dishwasher, power shower, computer, plasma TV . . . !

Sometimes we think our purchase is motivated by *need*, but in reality the main driver may be *want*. If we were genuinely motivated only by *need*, we'd buy very little. Most consumer spending is discretionary, not essential. We probably don't *need* more shoes if we already have 25 pairs sitting in the closet, but oh how we love those Jimmy Choos, and it's always useful to have a pair of smart shoes in the wardrobe just in case we have a posh do to attend! Same goes for the latest electronic gizmo. It probably does much the same as the earlier version that we already own, but we are happy to kid ourselves that what we want is also what we need – it will save time, we'll be more organised and efficient.

'Whether we're talking products or services, there's usually more to a purchase than mere utility value.'

Whether we're talking products or services, there's usually more to a purchase than mere utility value. Think about mobile phones. If our only interest was in the utility value – making calls, perhaps checking emails, surfing the Net, listening to music and taking the odd photo – there would be no need for so many different models, colours, cases, skins and other accessories, and we'd only ever replace a phone when the last one had died. We'd reach our purchase decision based solely on a rational evaluation of function. Style and fashion would not be a factor.

But most people are influenced by so much more than a sensible weighing up of pros and cons. Other factors come into play too, such as our social class, the effects of the media, peer and family pressure, our level of educational attainment, even how consumer-savvy we are: all play a part in what we buy, when, why and how. People are also heavily influenced by their social standing, political affiliations, values and beliefs.

A designer suit may be purchased to signal our good taste or social status; welly boots made from recycled African goat poo might serve to reinforce our environmental credentials or our ethical beliefs. Either way, they make a statement about who we are or what we believe in. There are people who buy a car simply to get them from A to B, but for many others their car says something about them, their attitudes and their lifestyle. Try selling products and services on utility value alone and you may struggle to make a sale. That's why you need to really understand what motivates your customers.

Impulse also features as a powerful purchasing force. Something looks fun, it's a bargain or it may be useful in some way, so we splash out without too much thought. Treats, indulgencies and gifts are another reason – the big box of choccies, the manicure, the weekend break, the toy train set . . .

Resale is another key reason for purchasing, with wholesalers buying from manufacturers to resell to retailers, to resell to customers.

Entertainment, too, can be a motivator, whether it's an MP3 music download, an opera ticket or a new paperback book. Then there's fear (burglar alarms), peace of mind (insurance), investment for the future (stocks and shares), because you're a collector (works of art, porcelain) . . . motivation comes in many shapes and forms.

Motivation is often multifaceted. A book might be bought on impulse, because the subject matter makes a statement about us, because a friend recommended it, because we like the author and also because we believe that it will be entertaining and educational. A restaurant meal has a certain basic utility value if we are hungry, but it may also be a treat and entertainment.

'Try selling products and services on utility value alone and you may struggle to make a sale. That's why you need to really understand what motivates your customers.'

What motivates your customers?

Think about your customers and what motivates them. Tick all of the following boxes that apply, and at the end of the list add any additional motivations that push your customers into buying your products:

☐ Need (specify) ………………………………...

☐ Utility value (specify) ………………………………...................................

☐ Impulse

☐ Gift

☐ Treat

☐ Resale

☐ Self-improvement/education/training

☐ Entertainment

☐ Investment for the future

☐ To satisfy our beliefs or values

☐ ....

☐ ....

☐ ....

Think about your answers to the above: were they based on guesswork, or on research? If it was the former, you will need to check that your guesses were accurate, by carrying out a little research to delve into your customers' motivations. We'll look at how to do this later in this chapter. For now, revisit the list and alongside each box that you ticked, try to allocate a percentage. If you think that your customers buy primarily for entertainment, how much of a factor is this? Fifty percent? Ninety percent? Is utility a motivation? What percentage would you assign it?

This is a useful exercise because it will help you to shape your sales messages. If utility value simply does not register as a motivation for your customers, there is little point in flagging it up in your sales pitches, presentations and marketing material. Once you know what motivates them, you can focus your efforts on drawing attention to those aspects of your product or service that are relevant for buyers.

Company A might consider buying your ergonomically designed desks because they place a high value on the comfort and wellbeing of their staff and recognise that your desks will guard against poor posture, back problems and will generally leave employees feeling fit and supple. Business B might be interested in buying because the vast range of colours that you offer complement their lovely, interior-designed premises. If selling to Company A, you would emphasise very different points than if selling to Business B. Each has a different motivating key. The obvious way to find the motivating key is to ask. The opening question: 'Why are you thinking about buying new desks?' allows you to start a conversation that will enable you to understand their motivator.

Left brain, right brain

Our decisions to buy are, of course, usually affected to a degree by logic – the objective evaluation of the pluses and minuses of a particular product – and also by emotion and desire (it's gorgeous, we covet it, we'd feel great wearing/ driving it . . .). Many people believe that the key to successful sales is twofold: first, you must persuade your potential customers to really want what you're selling (you must build desire) then you need to provide reasons to go ahead with the purchase (by appealing to their logic). That way, customers can justify giving in to desire by reciting all manner of logical reasons why their purchase was a good decision. 'It will save me money in the long run', 'It will be good for my health' or 'It's a great investment because it will last for years' are common justifiers used to validate a purchase.

It has been shown that when we make a significant purchase, we use both sides of our brain. We use the left side, the hemisphere in which logic resides, to analyse the information before us, evaluate the pros and cons, and examine the objective facts concerning a product's features. In short, we act in a sensible and rational way. But we also use the right side, the home of emotion and intuition. In some people the left side dominates the eventual decision, while in others the right side will prevail. If you are able to identify the side of the brain that dominates the customer standing before you, it will help you to sell to them by enabling you to focus primarily on logic or on emotion, and highlight the kinds of things that are likely to swing a sale.

When it comes to gender stereotyping, it's a no-brainer. Never assume that all women are right-brain people, while all men are left-brainers. That's one sure way not to make a sale! A left-brainer is generally very well organised, so they may well note down some questions to ask the salesperson, or bring with them a checklist of important product features that they require. They may come armed with information on what is available from competitors, or make notes while you are talking. Give them facts, figures, statistics, comparisons and other information that will help them to decide that your offering is the best. The

'It has been shown that when we make a significant purchase, we use both sides of our brain.'

left-brainer might want to go away and think about it before committing, allowing themselves time to carefully evaluate all of the information that they have gathered. They cannot be rushed into a purchase.

The right-brainer might comment on how nice a product looks or feels, or on style and design features, colour and shape. They might imagine themselves owning the product and fantasise about how that would feel. Pander to this and encourage them to sit in/on/try on/use the product. They are more likely to be impulsive and to make a purchase there and then, based more on gut feeling than on an objective evaluation of the facts. Nevertheless, they will need to be confident in the product, the salesperson and the company before they buy, so don't assume that selling to right-brainers is easy!

Take another look at the tick-box list on pages 23 and 24, in which you identified the factors that motivate your customers to buy from you. This time, think about left-brainers and right-brainers. What facts and features would you flag up if faced with a left-brained customer? What about a right-brainer? What is it about your products that will appeal to their spontaneity, impulsiveness and creativity?

> 'There are lots of different, cheap and easy ways to undertake market research and it's something that you should do regularly if you want to steal a march on your competitors in the cut-throat world of sales and selling.'

Market research

It's all very well to guess at what motivates your customers, but until you ask them, you will never know for sure what really lies behind their purchasing decisions. That's where market research comes in. If the term 'market research' conjures up images of ladies with clipboards and questionnaires, think again! There are lots of different, cheap and easy ways to undertake market research and it's something that you should do regularly if you want to steal a march on your competitors in the cut-throat world of sales and selling. Market research can tell you so much – not just what motivates your customers, important though that is – but a whole load more besides, all of which will ultimately help you to maximise sales. It can help you to find out more about:

- Your customers – Use research to find out who your customers are; what their main characteristics are; where in the town, country or world they live; what motivates them to buy; who else they buy from, when and why.

- Your products and services – Discover what customers think about your products and services. Are they happy with your offering? Are there any changes or improvements that they'd like to see? What would they like you to sell that is currently unavailable from your company? Knowing the answers to these questions will enable you to better meet customer need, which is a great way to sell a lot more.

* Your competitors – Do your customers buy from them too? What do they think of their offering? How does it compare with yours in terms of quality, price, speed of delivery, calibre of staff? What do their customers think of them and their products? Might they be willing to become your customers too? What can you learn from competitors that will enable you to improve your offering?

* Customer satisfaction – What do your customers think of you? Do they feel well served or badly treated? Do they recommend you to friends and colleagues or warn others not to buy from you?

Finding out about your customers is a good idea, but where do you begin? If you sell face-to-face, you'll already know a bit about your customers from your own observation – but there's bound to be more that you should find out. Equally, if you have a small but select customer base, you're likely to know your customers quite well, but a deeper understanding of them may help you to sell more to them and to others like them.

Desk research

Start with some 'desk research' – an analysis of data already in your possession, such as your invoices, sales records and website analytics. It's amazing what you can discover from information that you already hold, such as:

* The gender split of your customers.

* Which parts of the country or the world you serve.

* What the average customer spend is.

* Who your best customers are.

* What your most profitable products or services are.

* When sales' peaks and troughs occur – during the day, month and year.

- How often and when customers buy.

- Whether you have mainly regular customers or one-off purchasers.

- How many people visit your website, how long they spend there and how many go on to make a purchase from you.

- Which are the most popular pages on your website.

If you do not know the answers to these, time to get cracking on an analysis of your existing data. What can you find out and how might that knowledge help you to sell more profitably?

Aside from information in your possession, there's data out there in the wider world that you can access to help build up a picture of your customers and your competitors. Look at trade, technical, consumer and other relevant publications to find out about trade news for your business sector, to see what your competitors are promoting, to understand market trends and to generally create a good understanding of your marketplace. Pick up competitors' sales literature and attend trade events. Web searches are useful too. Visit competitor websites to see what they're offering and what they charge. Visit blogs and chat rooms to find out what consumers really think. Check out price comparison websites to see how competitive you are.

For a fee, you can obtain market data from some of the big market research companies. Many of them produce sector reports, such as retail or construction, which you may find useful.

Primary research

In addition to analysing the information that you already hold, and obtaining data that's already out there, there are other ways of finding out more about your customers and your competitors. It need not be rocket science and it need not necessarily involve an expensive external market research consultancy:

- Questionnaires – Send out a simple questionnaire by post or email, put one online or ask customers if they would be willing to complete one while they wait at your premises. As an incentive, include a prize draw.

- Observation – Observe customers shopping to understand more about how they act, or simply chat with them and learn more that way. You could watch a rival's premises to see how many customers visit during a set period and compare that with your own footfall.

- Focus groups – Ask a group of customers representative of your customer base to join you for tea and cupcakes, then ask for their views on your company, your products and services, your prices, their motivation for shopping with you . . . or anything else you want to find out about. Be clear about what information you want to find out, structure the discussion to cover these points, and have a note-taker to record the key points. Remember to write and thank participants afterwards.

Innocent, the smoothie company which has an annual turnover of £100 million, conducted some research in the early days of the business. The then two-man part-time business was trading at a small weekend event. At their stall were two large bins for empty cups, one labelled 'yes' and the other 'no', with a huge sign above reading 'Do you think we should give up our jobs to make these smoothies?' At the end of the weekend there were no complicated computations or mind-blowing mathematics required to work out the results of their research; they simply counted the cups in each bin and the rest, as they say, is history!

Market segmentation

By undertaking basic market research, you can begin to form a picture of your customers. Let's imagine for a moment that you manufacture and sell men's underpants mail order. A quick analysis of your sales records will reveal the gender spilt of your customer base. You might perhaps expect it to comprise mainly men, but what if 80 percent of your customers are female? Does this mean that your customers are women who like to wear men's pants? Unlikely! Delve further with a bit of primary research. Suppose a questionnaire sent out to customers, with a prize draw incentive to encourage a good response, uncovers the fact that you have three distinct groups of female customers: young women who buy their husbands' pants, older women who buy their husbands' underwear, and mothers who buy their grown-up sons' underpants. That's where market segmentation comes in. By segmenting the market into

'By undertaking basic market research, you can begin to form a picture of your customers.'

the clusters of customers with similar attributes and motivations, it becomes easier to tailor the product, the packaging and marketing activity from which sales are built.

A young woman buying pants for her partner might look for stylish, funky or sexy designs and natural fabrics, whereas an older woman shopping for her husband may place value on factors such as quality of workmanship, durability, comfort or perhaps price. The type of man who still allows his mother to buy his undergarments is very different to the kind of man who buys his own pants! Until you have identified your customer segments – and their particular characteristics, preferences and taste – you cannot successfully meet their needs and therefore cannot maximise sales. By categorising customers, you can achieve more sales, by:

'Until you have identified your customer segments – and their particular characteristics, preferences and taste – you cannot successfully meet their needs and therefore cannot maximise sales.'

- Targeting those groups more likely to be attracted to your products and services.

- Amending your products/services and packaging to meet the needs of your customers.

- Targeting advertising and other marketing activity so that it appeals to, and reaches, the right potential customers.

Research for business-to-business sales

Do you sell to other companies (B2B) rather than direct to consumers? If so, why not use research to help you find out a bit more about your customers. Desk research may tell you all you need to know, but don't rule out questionnaires and focus groups too. Suppose you run a small courier company. Your initial desk research has shown that 85 percent of your work comes from half a dozen big firms in town. There's little point in wooing the directors of those and similar firms if the decision as to which courier company to use is left to the secretaries. They should be your target. It is often only by undertaking research that you can really understand your customers – the companies themselves, and the influencers and decision-makers within them.

Do you really understand the companies that you do business with (and the ones you'd like to trade with)? Are you clear about who is the decision-maker within your various market segments? Do you really know what they are looking for from your company? Do you understand their buying process? Really? Then you'll be able to answer all of the following questions with confidence and accuracy:

※ Think of three companies that you currently don't do business with, who are on your hit list. Who (by name and job title) in each of the companies do you need to approach to arrange a B2B sales visit? How do you know for sure that that's the right person: the decision-maker?

※ Think about your top ten customers. How often does each of them buy what you are selling and what is their annual spend? Do they buy from you daily/weekly/monthly? Only at Christmas? Every four years? Do they buy only from you or from other suppliers too? (If so, who are your rivals?)

※ What and how long is the buying process for each of your top ten? (Do they buy routinely from the cheapest supplier when their supplies are almost depleted? Do they start considering the options and researching the market six months before a final decision is reached?)

※ What are the key dates in the buying process? (Is there a cut-off date after which they will not accept tenders or proposals?)

※ At what stage, if at all, can you influence the decision?

※ How does each company decide from whom to buy? (Do they consult a list of approved suppliers? Do they shop around for the best deal? Do they ask for formal tenders? Do they use personal contacts? Do they have one preferred supplier?)

※ Are there any constraints as to who they can buy from? (There is no point in spending time chasing a company that will only do business with companies whose turnover is higher than yours.)

※ How does each company reach a decision? By a formal appraisal of the options? By holding a meeting? By leaving it to one individual to decide?

※ Who will take the final decision as to whether/when/from whom to buy?

※ Who else may influence the decision?

If you struggled to answer any of the above, work out how you can find the answers. Could you take potential customers out to lunch and ask them some questions informally? Perhaps you could arrange a visit, not to sell, but to fact-find. Draw up a plan to build up a better understanding of your B2B clients and potential customers, then use that knowledge to widen your customer base and to sell more to existing customer.

The buying process

It is widely accepted that in many situations, the buying process comprises the recognition of a problem and the seeking of a solution, as you can see in the flowchart on the next page. Alongside, in the flowchart, you can see the opportunities for the salesperson to influence the buying process in a positive way in order to help secure a sale.

'It is widely accepted that in many situations, the buying process comprises the recognition of a problem and the seeking of a solution.'

In reality, consumers may or may not always identify a problem. Sometimes the salesperson presents a problem of which the customer may be unaware, then offers the solution. In this way, the consumer may never undertake an information search or alternative evaluation; they may just buy from you – if they can relate to the problem you have highlighted, have confidence in you and your suggested solution, and believe that you can provide it on acceptable terms.

Customer Behaviour	Salesperson Opportunity
	Customer may not recognise that there is a problem. Use marketing material or sales call to highlight the problem – and offer the solution!
Problem recognition: Customer sees a problem and wants a solution.	
Information search: Customer looks at what's available in the marketplace to solve the problem, or asks trusted sources.	Salesperson needs to ensure that company's website, advertising and other marketing materials are seen by potential customer.
Alternative evaluation: The consumer compares what's available and tries objectively to evaluate their pros and cons to reach a decision.	Salesperson highlights benefits in sales pitch or marketing material. If customer failed to identify initial problem, they may skip this step and accept salesperson's suggested solution – if powerful reasons provided.
Purchase decision: The consumer decides who to buy from, although this does not mean that any purchase will be made. The customer may not get round to it or may get cold feet.	The salesperson can encourage the sale to proceed by offering an incentive, easy payment or credit terms and so on.
Post purchase: The consumer is happy with the product and will buy from the company again, or is unhappy and will not do business with that company again.	The salesperson can contact the customer to check that they are happy, to resolve any problems and to demonstrate that the company cares – even after a successful sale.

Finding out why a customer didn't buy

It can be frustrating spending lots of time pitching to a client or wooing a customer only to see that effort not translated into a sale. Yes, it's disheartening, but don't let it put you off your stride for too long. Feel sorry for yourself by all means, but just for a minute or two, then stop wallowing and find out why it went wrong. (Remember that a successful salesperson is resilient and bounces back after a disappointment.) If appropriate, contact the customer by phone, post or email and politely ask if there was a problem – and if there was, see if you can resolve it. Again, if appropriate, ask if they purchased from elsewhere and, if so, why. Gather as much information as you can to help you understand where you may have gone wrong, or how a competitor got it right, and use this knowledge to help prevent you repeating your error in the future. Leave the customer feeling that although you were unable to do business together this time, they would like to talk to you again next time they're buying.

Common reasons for a salesperson failing to make a sale include:

'Leave the customer feeling that although you were unable to do business together this time, they would like to talk to you again next time they're buying.'

- The salesperson did not successfully demonstrate to the customer why they needed the product.

- The salesperson did not instil the customer with confidence in his/her ability or knowledge.

- The salesperson did not listen and respond to the customer's needs or concerns.

- The customer did not believe the salesperson's claims or didn't like his/her style or manner.

- The customer felt bullied, badgered or pressured into making a purchase and reacted against this by taking his or her custom elsewhere.

- The company has a poor reputation so the customer was unwilling to risk doing business with it.

- The price, product, terms, guarantees or after-sales support did not meet the customer's requirements.

If any of those apply in your case, you have some serious work ahead of you in strengthening your own selling skills, improving your company's reputation and putting together a package that meets your customers' needs. Start now!

Of course, there will always be times when you fail to achieve a sale for reasons that are beyond your control. Sometimes a customer simply doesn't buy in the end, or buys elsewhere for perfectly legitimate reasons. Classic grounds for customers choosing not to buy include:

- It is a big commitment and the customer needs some thinking time.

- It's a big commitment and the customer gets cold feet and decides to settle for what he/she already has.

- The customer is prospecting the market and may come back to buy in the near future, once they know what's available out there.

- The customer's circumstances have changed and it is no longer the right time to buy.

- There was nothing wrong with your product or service, but a more suitable offering was available elsewhere that more closely met customer need.

Follow up if you can, to understand why your sales pitch was unsuccessful. Try to leave the door open so that the potential buyer can approach you again should they change their mind or their circumstances.

Action points

■ Find out more about your B2B customers. List your five top clients, identify the key decision-maker in each, and take that person out for coffee or lunch. Be clear in your mind about what you want to find out from them. Ask about how they do business, when and with whom. Be careful not to interrogate, but just chat and let the conversation flow – making a careful mental note of anything useful.

■ Think of three really compelling things about your products or services that could create strong desire in your customers. Now think of three logical reasons why customers should buy your offering. Review your sales literature, sales patter and sales presentations to ensure that you have drawn sufficient attention to these points.

■ Analyse your existing data, then work out how you can use the findings to your advantage. For example, if you find that your mail order customers are mainly in the south east, consider attending a sales exhibition in the north, or placing ads in northern publications, to help build a customer base in a currently underexploited area.

Summing Up

- In this chapter we began by looking at some of the motivations that drive consumers to buy products and services – from basic need through to impulse and enjoyment.

- We learned that it's hard to sell things if all you ever flag up is the utility value. Then we discussed how to spot customers who are led by rational left-brain decision-making, and those who are more spontaneous and tend towards the right side of the brain.

- We moved on to examine how simple research techniques such as questionnaires and focus groups can be used to help you understand your customers a bit better, and how some basic market segmentation can help you to target your sales materials and sales messages more effectively.

- We looked at selling B2B (business to business) and how researching certain aspects of companies' buying behaviour, such as how often they buy and who is the chief decision-maker, can help you target them most successfully.

- We ended by reviewing the buying process, looking at how an effective salesperson can influence the customer at various stages. We also discussed why a salesperson may not always achieve a sale.

Chapter Three

Selling Face-to-Face: The Powerful Sales Presentation

Making a sales pitch is the part of selling that many people dread. Those who confidently and successfully sell one-to-one with complete ease can become nervous wrecks when they have to stand up and make a formal sales presentation to prospective clients. Sound familiar? Well, there's plenty you can do to build your confidence and ensure that your presentation is a success. The secret lies in good planning and preparation.

'Preparation builds confidence.'

Planning and preparation

If I asked you to get into your car right now, drive across the country and make a sales presentation to a company about which you knew nothing, you'd most likely feel a little anxious. That would be entirely understandable given that you would be unprepared, you may not have your presentation materials ready and you'd know nothing about the company and their requirements. You might even be in casual 'dress-down Friday' mode. All of these factors would contribute to your feeling of unease. Conversely, if you had quality materials ready, you'd done your homework on the company and you were dressed to impress, you would feel more comfortable about the challenge. Preparation builds confidence.

Start with yourself

Anyone who lacks confidence in themselves will inevitably find it hard to stand up and sell – because you're not only selling a product or service, you're effectively selling yourself too in that if your prospects don't believe in you, they won't believe in what you're selling.

To sell successfully, you must be comfortable with how you look and satisfied with how you come across. You need not be beautiful or handsome, ultra-confident, charming or showy. You simply need the right attitude and appropriate clothes. The right attitude is about being well prepared and showing eagerness, interest, enthusiasm and knowledge about your product or service and your company. It helps if you're also reasonably personable and likeable. Dressing for the part does not require expensive designer outfits; being well turned out for the occasion will suffice, so dress appropriately but comfortably. This is not a time for heels that you can't walk in or a suit that is so figure-hugging that you need to hold your belly in throughout the pitch!

'To sell successfully, you must be comfortable with how you look and satisfied with how you come across.'

Take a look in the mirror and decide whether you need to improve what you see. At the risk of sounding like your mother, are you well groomed with tidy hair, clean fingernails, polished shoes and ironed clothes? Could you smarten yourself up at all? Do you need to invest in a new outfit or a neat hairdo? You'd be surprised at how many shabby-looking people there are in business and if sales is your game, you simply cannot afford to be one of them yourself.

First impressions are important because you probably won't get a second chance. Research shows that first impressions are formed in the first two minutes. Urban folklore suggests that something like 40-55 percent of the first impression you make on others will be based on how you look. The way you speak accounts for 40 to 50 percent of your impact, while only seven or eight percent is based on what you actually say. Whether or not you believe that break down, it is a fact that you will make a first impression and you need to make sure that it's a good one.

Get back in front of the mirror, look at your reflection and smile at what you see. Practise this, because smiling when you greet someone is an underused yet easy and powerful way to make a great first impression and to help establish a good rapport. It also improves one's general appearance – and it costs nothing!

40

Do your homework

Before any sales presentation, smart salespeople always do their homework. Fail in that respect and you might as well stay at the back of the class with a dunce's cap on, because you're unlikely to make that sale. In preparing for your presentation, find out in advance:

- As much about the company as is relevant to your understanding of their needs. Visit their website and use a search engine to find out what others are saying about them. This background information will help shape what you say to them and will demonstrate that you understand their business sector. Also research your competitors, as they will likely be pitching too, and you need to know who and what you are up against.

- What the company is looking for and why. Tailor your presentation to address these points.

- Who will be at the presentation and what their position is within the company. Websites such as www.linkedin.com are useful for the potted profiles they provide of business people, so look up the CVs of those you will be pitching to and find out a little about their background. No harm in looking up your rivals too. What are their credentials?

- How much time you'll have. Prepare a presentation that is shorter than the allotted time, to allow for answering questions and queries, resolving any outstanding issues and possible negotiating.

- Who else (or how many others) are pitching. Your prospect may not be happy to share that information with you, but no harm in asking.

- What equipment will be available. (If you want to do a PowerPoint presentation, will you need to bring your own laptop and projector? Will there be a convenient plug socket?)

- How to get to the location of the presentation and whether there is any parking locally (there's nothing worse than arriving late and flustered from having lost your way en route or from searching for a parking meter).

Preparing your presentation

Being invited to make a sales presentation is a great honour. Your company has been selected to showcase its wares in front of people who want to buy what you are selling. Don't let a poor presentation spoil the opportunities on offer today and in the future, because remember that a poor presentation now may result in your company not being asked back in at a later date. Put time, care and effort into preparing a great pitch, one that will have impact, one that will lead to success.

Putting together a powerful presentation need not be difficult. Begin by working out your key messages. In the previous chapter we looked at some of the motivating factors that persuade people to buy your products. Do your research, understand what these factors are, and draw attention to them during your presentation. When drafting your presentation, flag up the things that are relevant to your prospects and cut out any unnecessary or irrelevant background information or detail.

'Be proud of what makes you different. Flag up your company's strengths or your product's unique features so that you stand out from the crowd.'

Remember that your audience want to know not only that you can supply what they are looking for, but also what makes your offering better than your rivals'. It's not usually a good ploy to criticise your competitors, as this makes you look small and petty, but by all means blow your own trumpet. Make sure that you have covered all of the benefits that you can provide. Be proud of what makes you different. Flag up your company's strengths or your product's unique features so that you stand out from the crowd.

To prepare the prefect presentation, just follow these simple steps below.

Ten steps to perfect presentations

1. Start by writing down your presentation as if it were a speech (but remember that you will never be reading it out verbatim!) By initially writing it up in this way, you can work out what you want to say, ensure that you have not omitted anything important, and organise a logical running order. Keep it natural, as you must be able to be spontaneous in response to questions and comments, but you also require a structure so that what you say has a logical order and covers the key points.

2. Turn your written 'speech' into a series of cue cards to act as aide memoires that will help you navigate your way through your presentation. Don't use too many cards; just enough to prompt you should you forget where you are in the running order. Number the cards so you can be sure that they are in the right order, and mark those that can be ditched if you are running out of time.

3. Write down any questions you are likely to encounter and, crucially, any objections that may be raised. Come up with responses and, as you see fit, incorporate these responses into your standard presentation to help avert queries and objections later.

4. Write down any questions that you would like to ask them. (See the list on page 46 for a few ideas.)

5. Rehearse your presentation in front of colleagues or family (or just a mirror or webcam), using your cue cards (not your speech) and take on board any comments your mock audience make about both content and delivery. Ask about any irritating mannerisms you have – such as repeatedly saying 'you know what I mean,' scratching your head or jangling coins in your pocket. These are often a sign of nerves. Make sure you have stopped doing these annoying things by the time of the real pitch.

6. Finalise your presentation in light of feedback, including adjusting the length to fit the time frame you have been given. Rehearse until you no longer need notes.

7. Prepare your PowerPoint presentation or any other visual aids that you plan to use.

8. Prepare a written document summarising the key selling points which you can leave behind with your audience. Make sure it looks great and that you have thoroughly proofread it.

9. Remember to personalise your generic sales presentations and sales material to the needs of each potential new client. It must never look generic, even if the core material is standard issue.

10. Anticipate well in advance any problems, issues or concerns that might arise during your presentation and work out how you will deal with them so that when the big day arrives, you can walk in confident that you will be able to handle whatever happens.

Dealing with nerves

It is natural to be a little nervous before a presentation, and it can even be quite helpful. The adrenalin that is a by-product of nervousness can fuel you through your presentation. But excessive shyness and nervousness will leave those to whom you are pitching ill at ease. They will not warm to you and your presentation will not go well. Getting on top of nerves is not difficult.

First, practise. If you are confident that you know what you want to say, you will be less nervous. Use card rather than paper for your cue cards, as paper has a tendency to shake if you are feeling nervous and it will attract other's attention to your jitters.

'Confident body language can conceal underlying nervousness.'

Work hard at pace. Too slow and you'll appear dull, sluggish and wooden. Too fast and you'll look nervous. Others will also find it hard to keep up with you. Perfect your pace during rehearsals and make sure that you don't suddenly speed up at the end to fit it all in. Work at developing your presentation skills and you'll find that your nervousness diminishes. Address any weaknesses that you have identified. If necessary, go on a course to improve your skills and confidence. When you finally come to make your presentation, remember to emphasise your strong points and make the most of them.

Control your body language

Confident body language can conceal underlying nervousness. If you look confident, people will believe that you are confident, and that will make you feel confident! Let's start at the top of the body and work our way down, beginning with the head. Keep your chin up, look around the room, make eye contact with everyone and smile. It will be impossible to smile throughout your presentation, and it would probably be inadvisable (you don't want to look like a grinning fool), but make sure that you don't frown or grimace. Maintain steady, deep breathing rather than the quick, shallow breaths of a nervous person. Stand tall and keep the shoulders and arms relaxed. Gesture by all means, but don't move like a windmill, with arms spinning about causing a distraction. Keep your hands out of your pockets and never fold the arms. Plant your feet firmly on the ground and don't shift nervously from one foot to the other.

Keep an eye on your audience's body language too, and pick up on any cues. They might sit there nodding and smiling (always a reassuring sign) or perhaps yawning and looking at their watch (rarely a good sign and always off-putting). Respond to these non-verbal cues. Speed up your presentation or abridge it if people look bored, or try a different tack and ask them a few questions to wake them up and involve them more. Never just bash on regardless of audience feedback.

The presentation

You have prepared your presentation and done your homework, you have taken steps to keep your nerves in check and now the big day has arrived. Take a deep breath then get on with it, confident in the knowledge that you can handle what's coming. The presenters of successful sales pitches:

'Keep an eye on your audience's body language too, and pick up on any cues.'

- Create a positive chemistry by smiling when they enter the room, offering a confident, friendly greeting and making good eye contact. The room lights up when they enter, not when they leave! They remember to introduce themselves and to explain (briefly) their role in the company. They may even ask the panel to introduce themselves if this courtesy is not proffered.

- Are lively and engaging. They use their voice to good effect, varying the tone and pace to maintain audience interest.

- Pitch their talk at the right level for the audience, avoiding over-technical explanations and using jargon only if they are confident that their audience will understand.

- Never try to make too many points in one go; they break up their presentation into separate points and give emphasis to each one.

- Always admit when they don't know the answer, rather than trying to bluff. (It is better to follow up afterwards with an accurate answer than to say something off the cuff that is untrue or inaccurate in response to a question.)

Making an impact

It is not uncommon at the start of a presentation for the audience to sit there looking stone-faced. Don't let this put you off your stride. They are not hostile; you would not have been invited if they were not interested in hearing from you. Smile, create a relaxed atmosphere and win them round.

Experts advise people to end their presentation on a high, but I'd advise to start it on a high too. If you start low-key and build up to a high, your audience may be lost en route. Grab their attention from the outset and keep it. Research has shown that the parts of any presentation that people remember best are the start and the finish. Use this to your advantage by really packing a punch when you open and again when you conclude.

A great way of holding attention is to encourage participation. Ask them questions, get them interacting with you and with each other. Let them play with, taste, handle or touch your products. Make it fun. Think about how you can bring a touch of theatre or showmanship to your presentation. You'll make it memorable and it will help you build a rapport with your audience.

Your sales presentation is an opportunity to present information, but remember that it's also a chance to gather it too. Make full use by asking open questions that will help you to fully understand what your potential customer is looking for and why. This will help you to shape your presentation to ensure that it fully meets their needs. Here are some questions that you might want to ask. Obviously you'll need to amend them to fit your own situation.

- What made you decide that you want to buy now?
- What do you hope this product can do for you?
- What is your budget for the project?
- What kind of challenges are you facing in your business, as there may be other ways in which we can help?
- What is important to you in a supplier?
- Is there anything about your current supplier or product that you are unhappy with?

Listen carefully to the answers and use active listening – nod, uh-huh and use other ways to demonstrate that you are listening and interested. If necessary, jot a few notes. As you progress through your presentation, make reference to the answers that you were given to the questions, to demonstrate how your company can fit the bill in terms of providing what the client is seeking.

A dozen deadly sins for sales presentation

1. Arriving late or allowing insufficient time to catch your breath, gather your nerves or set up the room/equipment.

2. Not preparing thoroughly, or not having all the necessary information or product samples with you.

3. Making a presentation that has no structure and leaves your prospective clients at a loss as to what you are trying to convey.

4. Delivering a generic presentation rather than a personalised one, and thus giving the impression that you simply can't be bothered.

5. Focusing attention largely on the principal decision-maker. This alienates others who may well have an influence on the final decision. If you do win the contract, you may well have to have future dealings with those you have alienated. Take an inclusive approach, involving everyone in the room.

6. Failing to modify the presentation you have prepared in response to audience reaction. Sticking rigidly to what you have prepared even when it is clear that parts of it are not of interest or irrelevant is a sure fire way to lose your audience. Create a 'chunked' presentation so that it's easy for you to drop a section if time or audience reaction are against you.

7. Talking in too much detail or for too long. Keep it snappy, lively and to the point. Too little information is rarely a complaint from those being sold to; too much is usually the problem!

8. Droning on in a flat, monotonous tone – especially if you are staring at your feet, your cue cards or your visual aids at the time.

9. Not listening or interrupting.

10. Not knowing the answers to questions that could have been predicted.

11. Failing to have a contingency plan in the case of equipment failure

12. Producing poor selling aids (such as tatty, dog-eared product information, grubby product samples or a PowerPoint presentation littered with typos or tacky clip art).

Visual aids

I did a sales pitch to a potential new client recently and afterwards they told me how nice it had been to see a presentation that did not rely on visual aids. I just stood up, talked with enthusiasm and asked questions. This made my pitch lively, natural and interactive – in stark contrast to my rivals, who bored the pants off everyone with their wooden performances in front of their laptop, using a bog standard PowerPoint presentation.

That said, there can be a place for visual aids during a sales pitch. Think about whether their use will add anything to your sales presentation. The following table, outlining the pros and cons of different types of visual aid, will help you work out what's best for you.

Visual Aid	Pros	Cons
PowerPoint presentation	It is useful for guiding you through the structure of your presentation. Simply work your way through the slides, with no need for cue cards. It is a good way of showing pictures of your products/services (if your product is not portable – such as large machinery or interior design 'befores' and 'afters'). It is easy to top and tail a standard presentation to tailor and personalise it for each new sales pitch.	It tends to be rather overused and predictable. It can be sleep-inducing for audiences – especially if the lights are dimmed. It can get in the way of proper interaction between you and your audicnce. It can be tempting to cram too much information into each slide. There is a danger of equipment malfunction, which can leave you lost if your presentation is dependent on it. It can be a bit formal if you are pitching to just one person rather than a panel of prospective customers. Poor presenters talk to the screen rather than their audience.

Visual Aid	Pros	Cons
Flipchart	It allows you to present in a more dynamic, interactive way than PowerPoint. It can accommodate off-the-cuff additions that you want to make.	It can be a bit cheap, tacky, informal or unprofessional-looking. You risk appearing as if you are running a training event rather than pitching for new business.
DVD	It can be a powerful way of showing your products/services in action using moving pictures. It can be a persuasive means of showing genuine satisfied customers and hearing their endorsements first hand.	If it lasts too long, you will lose audience attention; their mind will wander. It can be sleep-inducing, particularly if you lower the lights. It can be difficult and expensive to alter it for different sales pitches, so it can only deliver generic messages rather than specific ones tailored to each pitch. It can get in the way of proper interaction between you and your audience. There is always the danger of equipment malfunction.
Brochures and written material	It is useful to have key information and pictures pulled together in one reference document	As soon as you hand anything out, your audience will start to look at it rather than listen to you. (It's usually best to hand out such material right at the end of your pitch, so that they can look at it once you've left.)
Product samples	There's nothing quite like seeing for real the product that you plan to buy, and, if possible, sampling it. It's one thing to describe your catering service; quite another to come armed with a mini buffet!	It's not always easy to bring samples – they might be large or expensive – or you might provide a service that cannot easily be demonstrated during a sales pitch.

Reassuring and dealing with concerns

If you are presenting to a company with whom you have not previously done business, they might reasonably be a little sceptical about any claims you make. After all, if they decide to buy from you, they will be making a leap of faith when trusting in you, a possibly unknown quantity. Ensure that your presentation provides the necessary reassurance by clearly setting out your company's credentials (including testimonials from happy clients), your track record in the field, and real-life examples of how you have successfully helped similar organisations.

'Any claims that you make about your product or service, performance and so on need to be backed up with facts and figures, external endorsement or other data that will support what you are saying.'

Any claims that you make about your product or service, performance and so on need to be backed up with facts and figures, external endorsement or other data that will support what you are saying. Explain what you offer by way of after-sales support, including any guarantees. Ensure that they are not left with any reason to doubt your offering or your ability to deliver it, and no sense that doing business with you may pose a risk. Often companies stick with a tried and tested supplier because they are too afraid to chance taking on a new one that claims to offer better for less. Don't let their risk aversion hold you back, so anticipate their concerns and provide strong reassurance.

Dealing positively with concerns and objections

Questions, queries, concerns and even objections must be expected and planned for. It is natural that buyers will want to be sure that they are making the right decision, might wish to probe or might even have some reservations. Don't react defensively. You'll never make a sale that way. Nor should you feel defeated. Regard objections as a sign that the prospect is giving your pitch serious consideration but needs a bit of further reassurance before committing.

Acknowledge the validity of any concern by saying something like: 'Yes, I can understand why you might want to raise that.' Next, address their lingering doubts in a positive way. Listen carefully to the objection so that you fully understand what is worrying the prospect. Probe a little more if necessary before countering the objection in an upbeat way using facts and figures. Provide clear answers that show your openness and honesty; never waffle, avoid the question or give an inaccurate or untruthful response. Ensure that your answer addresses the specific concerns that have been raised. Summarising your sales pitch will not be sufficient.

If you have done your homework, you will already have spent time anticipating objections and devising positive responses to help allay any fears and deal positively with what might otherwise be a negative-ending encounter. Common objections you might well encounter include:

* You charge more than other suppliers. Why should we buy from you?

* We already have a supplier we are happy with. Why should we take the risk of switching to you?

* We can't afford what you are offering. It's a great product but it's just too expensive.

* We're worried that your company is not big enough to fulfil our order.

* Can you really guarantee the quality and consistency of your product time after time?

Have ready-made answers for these and other questions that you may be asked. One of the most common objections you will come across is that the customer already has a tried and tested relationship with another supplier. They will want powerful reasons for switching their order to you. You can address such an objection by suggesting that they try your service on a small scale to begin with, and once they are satisfied that you can deliver your promises, they can make a permanent switch. That way, you remove the risk element from the equation and make it easy for them to say: 'Yes, why not!'

Sometimes an objection might be perfectly reasonable, such as 'why should we buy from you when XYZ company is offering the same product at a lower price?' In such situations, throw the question back. 'We may charge very slightly more, but what you have to ask is this: can XYZ company guarantee the excellent levels of service that we can, including free delivery, loyalty discounts and first-rate after-sales support? A small premium for all of that extra value . . . ' Flag up what you can do better and re-emphasise your key selling points.

But even the best-prepared sales pitches may end with a query or objection that you could not have predicted. Don't let this throw you: keep your poise and handle it calmly and confidently.

Once you really understand your customers – how they think, what motivates them and what turns them off – you will be better placed to deal with any concerns or objections that they might have when you try to sell to them. Think back to the section on motivation in the previous chapter. When putting forward arguments to counter any objections, emphasise the points that motivate the customer; never spend time talking about things that are of no interest to them.

Although it is always best to address concerns there and then, if this isn't impossible – perhaps because you don't have the information to hand, or you don't have the authority to provide what is being asked for – there's nothing wrong with saying that you will need to check things out back at the office, and will respond to them within an agreed (short) timescale. It's not ideal, but it is better than bluffing and giving a wrong answer or making a promise that you cannot keep.

'As a matter of priority, make sure that you follow up undertakings that you made during your presentation.'

Post presentation

It can be tempting to heave a sigh of relief when the ordeal of making a presentation is over and slink back to the office with fingers crossed that your company will be selected. Don't! There is some important follow-up that you must do:

- As soon as you're back at base – or even before then – send an email thanking the company for the opportunity to pitch and expressing your eagerness for becoming their provider. Good manners cost nothing.

- As a matter of priority, make sure that you follow up undertakings that you made during your presentation. If you promised to call them with some further information, do so without delay.

- Spend a few minutes reviewing your performance. Could you have done anything better? How was your pace and timing? Did your visual aids work well or do you need to change anything? What might you do differently next time? If you presented as a duo or team, have a bit of a post mortem with colleagues – not to attribute blame if things did not go according to plan – but to learn from the experience and to ensure that next time it's even better.

If, after all that effort, that planning, that preparation, you get the news you've been dreading – you don't win the business – don't feel sorry for yourself or blame yourself (or each other). Instead, ask for some feedback so that you can better understand where you went wrong. Explain that you are disappointed not to win the business and that it would be useful to have some idea of the areas where you were weaker compared with the successful contender, so that you can make the necessary improvements. If you are given feedback, don't act defensively. See if you can learn from it, so that success is more likely next time. Be both resilient when it comes to criticism and open to new ways of doing things.

Soon afterwards, write saying that you were naturally disappointed not to be selected, but that you hope that things go well with their chosen supplier. This will show you in a good light. Emphasise in your letter that should any other opportunities arise in the future, you would be delighted to discuss these. This can sometimes lead to new business. I approached Need to Know, the publisher of this book, with a publishing proposal that was rejected. I followed up the rejection with a pleasant letter and a short while later they contacted me and suggested that I submit a proposal for a book on sales and selling – and you are now reading the result of that letter. So always be polite and make sure that their door remains open to you.

> 'Always be polite and make sure that their door remains open to you.'

A consultant I know sent an email recently to all of the businesses that he had unsuccessfully pitched to during the last two years. He asked whether there was any scope for working together in the future and he also requested honest feedback. This resulted in two new projects, four restored relationships and a lot of very nice emails in reply. He turned past failures into successes and you can do that too!

Action points

▨ Review any presentation materials that you regularly use and improve them.

▨ Make a list of at least half a dozen 'open' questions that you could ask during your sales presentation that would open up discussion and participation, as well as eliciting some useful information for you about the prospective company's needs and challenges.

- Write to or call companies you have pitched to unsuccessfully in the past and try to arrange to see them again. Tell them there have been exciting changes or improvements in your product range or your company that you'd like to share with them, then go in and deliver a lively presentation that will put your company back on their radar.

Summing Up

- In this chapter we looked at formal sales presentations, from how to plan and prepare for them through to how to deliver them with confidence and impact.

- There was advice on managing nerves and keeping a check on body language, and tips on things to avoid during a presentation.

- We also looked at practical ways of handling concerns and objections positively.

- We ran through what you need to check out before a presentation and things to follow up on afterwards, including advice on how to turn initial failure into future success.

Chapter Four

Words That Sell: Winning Sales Letters, Proposals, Websites and Adverts

There are lots of ways of selling. You can do it online by setting up a website, ensuring its search engine optimisation and relying on people to find you out there in cyberspace. You can hunt prospects down and cold call. You can keep an eye out for invitations to tender and respond with your sales document. You can wait for customers to walk into your premises, where you can sell face-to-face. You can advertise and sell mail order, produce flyers and mailings, email prospects . . . or more likely, your sales strategy will involve a combination of some or all of the above. In the last chapter we looked at selling face-to-face in the formal situation of a sales presentation. This chapter is all about *written* sales material – successful sales letters, powerful proposals, effective ads and wonderful web copy. You're going to learn how to sell even when you're not there in person with a prospect.

Penning sales material is a bit of an art form, and successful copywriters can earn big bucks writing winning words for ad campaigns, sales brochures and other marketing material. They know that a few well-chosen words can transform a cold contact into a repeat purchaser – and they know exactly which words to choose. Let me share a few of their secrets with you so that you too can perfect that art and start penning powerful publicity. We'll start with direct mail or, as I like to think of it, selling through the letterbox.

'A few well-chosen words can transform a cold contact into a repeat purchaser.'

Direct mail: selling through the letterbox

Direct mail is a fantastic way of reaching out to new customers, or of getting lapsed customers buying again. It can even keep loyal customers up to date with your new product lines or special offers – and all for the cost of a stamp. Many companies rely on direct mail for sales. Even a one-off mail campaign can boost sales not just now, but into the future, by expanding your customer base.

Sounds good! But if you fancy a slice of it, beware the pitfalls too. Success isn't guaranteed and a large, unsuccessful mail campaign may prove expensive. So before you set off down that path, take note of these insider tips to help ensure success.

'Direct mail is a fantastic way of reaching out to new customers, or of getting lapsed customers buying again.'

When a customer receives a mailshot through the post, they will look at the envelope; open it (if you are lucky); read the contents (if you are really lucky); and place an order (if you are exceptionally lucky). On the other hand, they might just chuck it in the bin unopened. There are multiple opportunities for your hard work to be thrown away, a somewhat depressing thought. And there seems to be an ever diminishing chance that the recipient will progress to the stage of placing an order. I used the word 'lucky', but in fact luck has nothing to do with it. If your mailshot is thrown away unopened, it's not due to bad luck; no, it's because of bad targeting or inappropriate packaging. If it's unread, poor targeting or poor copy is to blame . . . Reader reaction is not a matter of luck but of careful planning. It's a potential minefield, but one that can easily be navigated.

The envelope

To guarantee a sale, the first challenge is to get the envelope opened. You'll improve your chances if you think of the envelope not just as a container, but as an integral part of the sales pitch. Decide whether to use:

- Plain white envelopes, manila envelopes or specially designed and printed envelopes bearing a sales message.

- Handwritten addressing or printed details.

- Normal format envelopes such as C4, C5, C6 or DL or unusual sizes, shapes or colours.

How can you increase the chances of your envelope being opened? Specially printed envelopes enable you to carry a powerful sales message to tempt your recipient to open the mailing. Such messages can be:

- **Urgent** – 'Open now to save £500' or 'Great offers inside, but hurry – stocks are limited' or 'Open now – time-sensitive offer!' Create a sense of urgency not only to encourage the reader to take a peak, but to do so immediately. Letters that sit in the in-tray for too long are less likely to be opened.

- **Intriguing** – Many people are dismissive of what they see as 'junk' mail and may be disinclined to open what you send them. Make your recipient feel intrigued by what may be inside your mailing. Unusual or intriguing envelopes can achieve this – perhaps something psychedelic, or an envelope with a vintage feel from a nostalgic era. Anything a bit different or unusual can work. Or print an intriguing message such as 'If only Tina had known!' You can explain your intriguing statement inside the mailing.

- **Incomplete** – A sentence begun on the envelope can be completed as part of the headline of your enclosure. 'Sally saved over £300 on her heating bills this year . . .' continued inside with 'by installing our double glazed windows'. (Never use this technique for business mailings, as secretaries often open mail and discard envelopes before passing the contents on to the addressee.)

- **Informative** – An informative statement printed on an envelope enables you to convey a message even if the envelope's never opened: 'The biggest furniture store this side of the Pennines'. Such an awareness-building message may influence the recipient at some later date, even if they fail to open this particular mailing.

The enclosures

Congratulations. You've clambered across the first hurdle: your mailing has been opened. Now it must be read. Your envelope will most likely contain a sales letter or some other covering letter and possibly an enclosure, such as:

- A catalogue, brochure or sales leaflet.

- An order form or reply card.

- A product sample or money-off voucher.

The covering letter

When there are other enclosures, the covering letter acts as navigator, explaining to the recipient what else is enclosed and why. If the letter is the only enclosure, its importance becomes greater as there is no glossy brochure or free sample to do the selling for you.

The main types of covering letter are sales letters (see below), which aim to get the recipient to place an order as a direct result of the mailing; and lead-generating letters, designed to get the reader to express an interest in your product or service, but not necessarily to buy there and then. For example, you might offer to put the recipient on your mailing list, enter their name in a prize draw, encourage them to send off for a money-off coupon or a free sample. At this point you are merely trying to get them interested in what you have to offer, and you can follow up later with a more direct sales pitch. The lead-generating letter weeds out those who are not serious buyers, leaving you with warm prospects to woo. Keep them fairly short, as there's no need to go into too much detail at this stage: all you are doing is asking someone to show an interest, you are not trying to sell just yet.

'Sales letters must engage the reader right from the off.'

Sales letters

Sales letters must engage the reader right from the off. If you lead in too gradually, beginning with the background information, progressing through the letter with detailed information, and ending with the offer, guess what? It might be a clear and logical way to write, but you'll have lost your reader well before they reach the main part of your letter: the offer. Turn logic on its head by starting with the offer and backfilling with detailed information. Hook 'em first by telling them that they can be richer, more youthful, sexier, more successful, have cleaner washing or faster broadband . . . then explain how.

Helpful hooks include the:

- Problem solver – 'Banish pimples and spots'.
- Fantastic offer – 'Quite simply the best Italian food you've ever tasted, or your money back!'

60

- 'Sit up and take notice' statement – 'Double your employees' productivity in just five days'.

- Amazing fact – '99% of other widget machines break down in their first year. Ours rarely break down in their entire lifetime'.

- Question you can't ignore – 'Want to know how to drop a dress size in just one week – without dieting?'

- Real-life story – 'When Paul left home for work that morning, the last thing on his mind was . . .'

- Direct comparison – 'Many companies the same size as yours operate more efficiently with far fewer staff'.

- Free gift or other incentive – 'Buy now and we'll send you this lovely pair of sewing scissors absolutely free'.

- Nostalgia – 'Remember when mobiles were the size of a house brick? When you wouldn't be seen dead in a jacket without shoulder pads? When girls danced round their handbags to Heaven 17? You do? Then you'll love our 1980s' night, first Friday of the month at the Meadowhead Hotel!'

- Testimonial – 'Since my first consultation last month, my skin is noticeably smoother. The fine lines have disappeared completely and skin tone is more even. In fact, I'm so pleased with the results that I've thrown my foundation away! And friends have complimented me on how youthful and dewy my complexion is'.

- Endorsement – 'The only machine to have won five consecutive gold medals from the British Association of Widget Makers'.

- Strength in numbers – 'Over 2,000 small businesses in the Midlands already use our . . .'

- Independent survey or test results – 'According to the government's own statistics . . .'

- Reappraisal – 'Think you can't afford a car like this? With our easy payment plans, you can!'

Irresistible openers like these leave readers wanting to know more. Now you're ready to give the detail. You're not selling products or services; you're selling solutions, so flag up the benefits of your product. Explain how your product or service can solve problems. Pay careful attention to how you present your proposition. You may need to do more than state the facts.

> Factual wording: '10-litre mineral water bottles for water coolers, £10 (ex-VAT) for a box of six.'
>
> Pacy proposition: 'Keep your staff fresh and hydrated this summer! Six 10-litre bottles of refreshing mineral water delivered free direct to your workplace for just £10 (ex-VAT). Suitable for all standard water coolers.'

'You're not selling products or services; you're selling solutions, so flag up the benefits of your product. Explain how your product or service can solve problems.'

Paint a picture of the benefits of the product. Throw in a few adjectives to help conjure up an image, but don't get carried away and drift off into over-flowery prose.

If it is a good deal, spell it out. In the examples above, the first fails to mention free delivery, yet that's a real selling point. Who wants to waste time and effort carting heavy bottles back from the supplier when they can get them dropped off at their premises totally free and gratis? Never assume that the reader will know, or that they'll go to the trouble of checking. Serve up any good deals on a plate.

I recently booked a cruise for my family and two weeks later received a letter from the cruise operator telling me that regrettably some necessary changes had been made to my booking, outlined in the enclosed documentation. I was advised that if I was unhappy with the changes, I should contact my travel agent. After poring over the enclosed document and comparing it with the original, I finally worked out that we had been put in different cabins to those booked – superior cabins. How much better if the letter had flagged up the great news: 'We're delighted to tell you that we've given you a complimentary upgrade!' Sales letters can also miss this trick by failing to shout out the good news or great offers.

Sales letter dos and don'ts

- Do offer a 'get out clause' wherever possible to reassure readers that it is safe to buy, such as 'Buy with confidence! Simply return your purchases to us in their original wrapping within 14 days if you're not 100% satisfied and we'll give you a full refund'.

- Don't make open-ended offers. Set a deadline to create a sense of urgency and to prod your recipient into action: 'Hurry. Offer ends on August 2nd!' Encourage responses with a 'speed incentive' such as: 'Reply by July 1st and save 10% on your order'.

- Do highlight anything that may clinch the deal, such as special prices, easy payment terms, free delivery or guarantees.

- Don't make it hard for readers to respond. Enclose a postage-paid return envelope, an easy-to-complete coupon or your web address so that they can order with ease.

- Do try to keep it short and sweet – ideally one sheet of paper. If you go on to two sides, end page one with a split sentence to encourage the reader to turn the page.

- Don't use the 'third person' (the customer, the company, buyers). The first person (you, me, our, us, etc.) is more direct and more personal.

- Do use everyday words, especially in sales letters to the public. You can get away with a bit of industry jargon in B2B mailings, but only if you are sure that the reader will be familiar with it too.

Sales letter ingredients

Every sales letter should have a:

- Beginning – The hook.

- Middle – Further detail about the proposition.

- End – A summary of what recipients need to do next, such as 'Remember that orders need to be with us by the end of the month if you want to take advantage of these special prices' or 'Visit our website today for our latest offers'.

Also consider using a post script. A handwritten style PS stands out from the rest of the text and can be used to reinforce the offer or encourage action: 'Hurry! This offer is only available until . . .' or 'Remember that our sale stock disappears fast!'

Powerful proposals

Your company may be invited to prepare a sales proposal or a competitive tender document setting out for the prospective customer what you can offer and on what terms. This kind of selling, where a document has to do the talking for you, can be difficult to write, because there's so much to say and always that lingering fear that you may omit something really important – a possible deal-clinching detail. However, resist the temptation to cram it all in. The recipient will have other proposals to read too, and if yours is text-heavy, and contains too much irrelevant background information or too much detail, it may be off-putting. Your prospect may resort to skim-reading it, with the danger that they then miss key information, or they may simply give up and turn to a rival's more concise documentation.

The trick with sales documents is to:

'Never allow your reader to have lingering doubts; leave them feeling that they can confidently do business with you risk-free.'

- Get the balance right – Not too much detail, but not too little. Work out what is essential information, what is desirable, and what can be ditched without any real loss.

- Get the style right – Convey a sense of the personality of your company and what makes you different from the others.

- Get your research right – Speak with the company on the phone and get as much information from them as possible about what they are looking for. Tailor your document to cover these key points.

- Get the offer right – Consider offering special terms on an initial order, or some other incentive to make your proposal more attractive than a rival's.

Just as when you are pitching face-to-face, so too with a sales document, anticipate likely objections or concerns and address them. Never allow your reader to have lingering doubts; leave them feeling that they can confidently do business with you risk-free.

Find out, if you can, how a decision will be reached. Will shortlisted companies be invited in for a face-to-face meeting, or will the decision-making be a purely paper exercise based only on the written documentation? How will the tenders or sales proposals be scored? What criteria will be used for scoring? Use this information to help you structure your document. Make sure that you cover all of the areas the prospective company has asked you to cover. Include samples if you can, or examples of how you have helped similar companies, 'before' and 'after' shots if applicable, or anything else that helps demonstrate the impact of your product or service. Back up any claims with hard facts, external endorsements and passionate testimonials.

Ensure that your documentation is perfect – no typos, grammatical errors or spelling mistakes; and no coffee stains or dog-eared corners. Bind it so that it does not fall apart on arrival. Use colour if possible. Use pictures, diagrams or illustrations where appropriate. Include as many copies as were requested. If no figure was stated, call and ask.

Contents checklist

Make sure that you include:

- A brief summary of your company and its credentials – length in business, key achievements, client list (if appropriate), awards or accolades etc. Don't get bogged down in irrelevant detail: 'We were established on July 16th 1997 . . .' Instead: 'Established for nearly two decades, we now . . .

- Everything that the prospective client requested.

- Your product's key selling points – stress the benefits to the client, rather than just the features (more on this in chapter 6).

- Answers to any likely objections.

- Powerful facts and figures (with sources).

- Independent endorsements, impressive testimonials and favourable press coverage.

- Any photos or graphical representations to help make your case visually attractive.

- Any necessary information about terms of business, guarantees, returns and so on that will be required at this stage.

Winning web copy

The growth of the Internet has created wonderful new opportunities to reach a geographically wider customer base. Small specialist companies can now sell not just locally, but nationally and even globally, thanks to the Net. It doesn't matter that you operate from a grubby workshop on an obscure industrial estate: if your website looks the biz, you can create the impression that your company is as good as anyone else's – and so long as you live up to your claims, your company is indeed as good as the next one! So why not profit from the great leveller that is the Internet. In cyberspace you can be the equal of big household names if you get your site right. The difference is that when you're up against the big boys, their advantage is reputation. They are a tried and tested name. No offence, but your small business might be a bit of an unknown, and given how many con websites exist, the hurdle you face is how to convince new customers that you are bona fide.

'The growth of the Internet has created wonderful new opportunities to reach a geographically wider customer base.'

If someone has not done business with you before, and they find your company through a search engine or comparison website, they might initially be wary of placing an order. After all, how do they know that you're not a front for some kind of scam? Allay their fears by:

- Linking to relevant bona fide websites such as your trade or industry body.

- Featuring endorsements or favourable comments from independent sources.

- Publishing a named contact, postal address and telephone number so wary customers can check you out before placing an order.

- Keeping your site up to date so that it appears to be an active enterprise rather than a dormant business. If your Christmas offers are still up in January, or your facts and figures are well out of date, it could put potential customers off.

Chances are that you'll already have a website, but if not, it can be somewhat daunting trying to work out what you need to include in order to secure sales. Take a look at your leading competitors' sites and see how they have tackled the problem. If you were a buyer rather than a seller, what would you like about their sites? What works and what doesn't? What about the big players in your market? Can you learn anything from them too?

Most websites include most of the following:

- A home page – The main navigational page of the site.

- About us – Company history and credentials.

- Products and services – Product/service details/specifications, pictures, information, special offers.

- News or What's New – The latest on your company, products or events.

- Contact us – Details of how to get in touch, including an enquiry form and a map/details of how to reach your premises.

- Site search – Some sites have a facility to search for keywords or products.

- Terms and conditions – Any small print.

- FAQs – Frequently asked questions (and their answers).

When selling via the Web, let pictures do the talking. If you have products to show, illustrate them with high-quality photos. Add short descriptions about sizes, materials, prices, product specifications, variants, alternatives and so on. Let viewers zoom in to see the detail of what's on offer. Cross reference so that shoppers can see that people who bought the product they are viewing also purchased the matching scarf.

Search engine optimisation

It's all very well having a great selling site, but the challenge is to get people to find your site from among the millions of others. This is where search engine optimisation comes in. When someone is looking to buy what you sell, what words are they likely to key in to a search engine to find your products? Suppose I was looking for a local venue to have a wedding reception. I'd probably type in 'wedding venues Edinburgh' or perhaps 'upmarket wedding venues, central Scotland'. List all of the words or phrases people might use when looking for your products or services. If I wanted a venue, its location would be vital. But if I wanted to order a book mail order, the location of the bookstore would be irrelevant to me (so long as it was UK-based). Consider whether your location is a keyword or not.

This is where it gets techie and you might need a little external help. Search engine optimisation consultants can help ensure that when people type those keywords into a search engine, your website pops up and traffic is driven to it. For a reasonable fee, you can get your site optimised so that people can find your site with ease when looking generally for a supplier of your products or services. This can have a big impact on sales. See *SEO: The Essential Guide* (Need2Know) for more information.

Talking of techie, how do you know if your web strategy is working? Well, apart from the obvious – sales generated by your website – you can also measure web activity using web analytics software. This will allow you to know how many people visited your site and where they came from, when and how often they visited, whether they looked at just one page or many, how long they spent there and all manner of other useful information. Armed with this analysis of visitor behaviour, you can amend your site to maximise sales.

'Make your ads memorable by being attention-grabbing. Once you have the reader's attention, hold on to it with interesting copy. Keep it short, snappy, lively and direct.'

Effective ads

Most small businesses can't afford the high costs of TV ads or national newspaper campaigns, but many advertise in trade publications, specialist magazines and the local media. It might just be a small classified ad, but it can still be an important tool to generate sales. Every effective ad attracts attention, promotes interest, generates desire and prompts action. This is summarised in the term AIDA.

AIDA (attention, interest, desire, action)

We see literally hundreds of sales messages every day: we remember only seven! Make your ads memorable by being attention-grabbing. Use powerful images, an arresting headline, vibrant colour, strong design or some other device to make your ad leap from the page and get noticed. However, don't use naked or semi-clad women to do the job for you: it's cheap and tacky, it causes widespread offence, and it's just not very 21st century.

Once you have the reader's attention, hold on to it with interesting copy. Keep it short, snappy, lively and direct.

Stimulate a desire to buy your products or use your service. Paint a picture of how it will change lives, create time, make things easier, brighter or better. Sell an idea or a dream. For example, if you were selling lipstick you may focus on beauty or attractiveness rather than product features such as ingredients or price. Leave your reader feeling that they simply must have one.

Great! They want it. Now make them buy it, because all the desire in the world is worth nothing if it's not translated into sales. Prod them into action. Tell readers what action is required:

- 'Call today to place your order'.
- 'Return the coupon for our colour catalogue'.
- 'Email sales@megasales.com for a free sample'.
- 'Pop into our giant store in Birmingham for the biggest range of sofas in the Midlands'.
- 'Visit our website for the latest offers'.
- 'Complete this form today to qualify for this special subscription offer'.

Advertising dos and don'ts

- Do use colour. Full colour ads in mags attract twice the readership of black and white ones.
- Don't forget to include a line space between paragraphs. It increases readership by 12 percent.
- Do consider using a heavy dashed border around small ads, giving the appearance of a coupon. It increases responses.
- Don't use too much unbroken text or small print. It is off-putting, difficult for anyone with eyesight problems and may give those who do tackle your text a headache.
- Do use good quality photographs, as research shows that they have greater credibility than other illustrations and generate about 25 percent more recall.
- Don't forget when using a coupon response to place a small code in the

bottom corner so you can tell which publication, or which edition of it, generated the response. This will help you to work out where and when to advertise for maximum sales.

- Do put body text *below* your photograph rather than above it. As the eye automatically lands on the illustration, any copy above will require the reader to have to read up to reach it. This feels unnatural.

- Don't waffle. Get straight to the point using short sentences and short paragraphs.

- Do use the first person – lots of 'we', 'you' and 'us'.

Hard-working headlines

'There's nothing more damaging to reputation (and future sales) than poorly fulfilled orders.'

The headline is one of the most important parts of your ad, so make sure yours works for you. Ineffective headlines lose 80 percent of readers. Those readers are your potential customers, so don't let them get away! Here are some ideas to help you get started with sales-boosting advertising:

- Use 'why' headlines – 'Why your rivals already have an XYZ widget machine'. This will leave the reader wondering and wanting to know the answer.

- Use 'how' headlines – 'How to get a better night's sleep'.

- Use 'do' headlines – 'Do you want to improve productivity in your office?' Make sure the answer to the question is always a 'yes'.

- Use a signpost headline – Alert your intended audience that this ad is aimed at them. 'Calling all chocoholics'. Those who hate chocolate will take no notice, which is fine, but chocolate lovers will want to know more.

Be ready to respond

You have posted your sales letters or placed your ads, all in the hope that the orders will flood in. Are you geared up to cope with the response swiftly and efficiently? There's nothing more damaging to reputation (and future sales) than poorly fulfilled orders. Make sure:

- You have enough employees available to answer the phone, to process orders and staff your premises.

- You have enough stock to respond to orders.

- Your staff know about your sales campaign and have all of the details to hand to deal with enquiries professionally.

Action points

- Visit rivals' websites to see how they approach sales. What things do they do on their website that you could copy? Visit other sales websites that operate in a different industry or area and see what you can learn from them too.

- Review any ads that you have placed over the last 18 months and check that you are making the most of this sales opportunity. Make sure that the headline works, that the body copy is snappy and that the layout attracts attention.

- Start setting aside any direct mail you receive over the next couple of weeks, both at work and at home. What tricks do other companies use to get your attention and to sell to you? Could you apply any of these tricks in your mailshots?

Summing Up

■ This chapter looked at some of the key ways of selling when you are not face-to-face with your customers, namely sales letters and other mailings; sales documentation and tenders; selling online; and press advertising.

■ We looked at simple ways to sell more effectively using the written word.

■ Tips included the importance of keeping sales patter short and snappy, flagging up key selling points early on, using powerful photos and illustrations, and being ready to respond to successful sales campaigns by having sufficient staff and stock to fulfil orders.

Chapter Five

Selling at Events, Trade Fairs and Exhibitions

Is selling at fairs, exhibitions and events a part of your sales strategy? Or would you like it to be? Then read on. Special events offer a wonderful opportunity to sell to people who are looking to buy, but they cost a lot too – in time as well as hard cash – so you need to be sure that you're going about it the right way to avoid wasting money and to maximise sales.

Setting objectives and choosing a showcase

First decide what you want to achieve from being at an exhibition or other sales event. Do you want to make sales there and then, or generate leads to whom you can sell at a later date? Or do you want to network and make useful contacts for the future? (If the latter, consider whether it would it be more time and cost-effective to attend as a delegate rather than an exhibitor.)

Be specific about your objectives. Is there a certain amount of stock that you would like to sell? Or a set number of leads that you would like to find? By having objectives, you can later assess whether or not the event was a success.

Once you're clear about your objectives, find the ideal event – one that your potential customers will attend in sufficient numbers for you to achieve your sales goal. Event organisers should be able to send you visitor and exhibitor profiles so that you know who will be there selling as well as buying. This is useful background information, but nothing beats first attending the event as a punter to get a sense of whether or not it is the right one for your company.

'By having objectives, you can later assess whether or not the event was a success.'

There's nothing more disheartening (or money-wasting) than exhibiting at an event where the exhibition hall resembles a graveyard. Good footfall is essential, so ask the organisers for exact figures from previous years. Also ask questions about how the event will be promoted to ensure good attendance. Which media will be contacted? Have any features or media coverage been secured? Request copies of media coverage from recent events. Ask also about publicity mailings: how many will be sent out, when and to whom. Find out about advertising: when, where and how often. Satisfy yourself that the organisers will work hard to draw in the target audience.

The practicalities

Once you've booked, check out the practicalities that will make things run more smoothly on the big day. Find out:

- What the set-up and take-down schedules are.

- Which loading bay to use to offload stock and furniture/props for your stand.

- What can be stuck to the exhibition shell and using what adhesive.

- The security arrangements if you have to leave the stand set up overnight with valuables on display.

- Your insurance liability (your goods may not be insured once they are off your premises. Check that they are covered by the organiser's insurance, or make alternative arrangements if necessary).

- When the text for your entry in the show catalogue is due. Don't rush it, as it's a first-class selling opportunity. Use lively copy that will attract people to your stand. Flag up any show special offers that will entice visitors.

Draw up a checklist itemising everything you need to do before, during and after the exhibition, including everything you need to bring with you. Forget one small but crucial thing and it could spoil an otherwise well-planned event. Be wary of assumptions. Never assume that Gayle is bringing the product information, Surinder will come with the products and Tom will organise the coffee. Unless you've briefed them and given them task lists, you can't assume anything. Ensure you assign each task, however small, to a named person. Don't forget to check that any equipment that is required – a DVD player or lighting, for example – is working, that everyone knows how to use it, and that you have contingency plans for equipment failure, such as spare bulbs and fuses.

Remember to tell your customers and warm leads that you are exhibiting. Invite them to visit your stand, perhaps by offering them an exclusive gift if they do so. Send a few free tickets if you think that will attract an important potential customer.

Counting the cost

Exhibiting for the first time almost always costs more (and takes up more time) than you expect. Work out costs very carefully, to help you assess whether or not you'll see a return on your investment. There are many costs to factor in, such as:

▨ Your stand/booth. Some venues charge per square metre of space occupied, or you may be given a space and told how big a display you can have on it. Some charge a premium for prime spots in the hall; others have a flat fee, so there's benefit in booking early and reserving the best pitch.

▨ Any additional/hidden charges for a PA system, stand lighting, electricity, equipment hire, extra rooms (for workshops or talks), extra seating or other furniture. Check carefully to see what will be provided, and whether it's OK for you to bring in your own seating or equipment.

▨ Stand decoration – including backdrops, exhibition/display boards (design and production).

▨ Any samples, giveaways/freebies you plan to hand out.

▨ Travel and accommodation for you and other staff if the event is away from home.

▨ Overtime costs (including setting up the night before and taking down afterwards).

▨ Temporary staff (or overtime) costs to work on your stand or to cover output back at base if key staff are tied up at the exhibition.

▨ Additional insurance if necessary.

▨ Materials such as brochures and product packs.

'Remember to tell your customers and warm leads that you are exhibiting.'

Don't forget to negotiate the price of your exhibition space. Even if there is no scope for a reduction, there may be other ways of getting a more favourable deal. If you have to pay full price, ask for free lighting, extra free tickets, a more prominent entry in the catalogue or some other compensation that will be valuable to you while costing the organiser little or nothing.

Sometimes companies may just break even, or even make a small loss, yet still decide to exhibit because:

- Being there allows them to reach an important and influential audience.

- They can make useful contacts from whom future sales may be secured.

- Some of the expenditure will have a long shelf life, such as display boards.

- Not being there may send out negative signals to customers and give rivals something to gossip about.

Your stand

'Incorporate some activity, movement or demonstration on your stand, as research has shown that this attracts more visitors than static displays.'

Your stand must be perfect. An amateurish, shabby or boring stand will not attract visitors and will send out negative messages about your business. Some companies employ designers to plan and create their space. If funds don't run to this, don't worry. You can still make a strong visual impact with a clean, uncluttered stand complete with attractive backdrop, eye-catching display boards and carefully displayed product samples. Coffee, a small seating area, a pretty bunch of fresh flowers, a plate of cookies or a dish of sweets and some marketing material add the finishing touches. Do everything you can to make your stand attractive, welcoming, and eye-catching. Plan your stand's layout so that it is easy for passers-by to stop and take a look or pick up a leaflet. Don't block the entrance with staff or tables, or make it too narrow. People don't want to have to negotiate an obstacle course to get to see your products.

- Incorporate some activity, movement or demonstration on your stand, as research has shown that this attracts more visitors than static displays.

- Consider offering free coffee at your stand. The aroma is pleasant, it is cheap to supply, and if served in ceramic mugs and not paper cups, people will not wander away to another stall until they have finished.

- Ensure that if you use a gimmick to entice visitors to your stand, it will attract the right people. There's no point in getting queues of punters if the vast majority just want the freebie.

Staffing your stand

An exhibition stand is no place for shrinking violets. Pick your sales team carefully, making sure that everyone is confident, personable and thick-skinned – but never pushy. Brief the team in practical ways of striking up a rapport with prospects. Some of your staff may be naturally good at engaging complete strangers in conversation, so play to their strengths. Deploy staff according to their special abilities. Those who are good at demonstrating products should undertake that role.

When someone approaches your stand, make eye contact, smile and immediately engage them in conversation. If you don't grab them quickly, they'll move on to the next stand. Never try to open up a conversation with 'Can I help you?' because the answer is almost always 'No, it's OK. I'm just looking' followed by a rapid exit. Devise an opening line likely to induce conversation, not kill it. Also avoid greetings such as 'How are you today?' The reply will be 'Fine, thank you,' again followed by a hasty retreat. Instead, ask a direct, open and relevant question that will make visitors feel comfortable and at ease:

- 'What are the key features you are looking for in your replacement widget machine?'

- 'What information can I give you about our new range of park benches?'

- 'What are you hoping to get out of today's exhibition?'

- 'Would you like to double the productivity of your staff?' (This is actually a closed question, but one that's hard to answer in anything but the affirmative!)

Treat every visitor to your stand as an individual. Do this by listening carefully and tailoring your response. If you launch full frontal into a standard sales spiel, your visitor will feel assaulted. Be sensitive to whether or not someone wants to talk, by watching their body language and looking out for other clues. Some visitors will be paper-collectors, picking up every leaflet and brochure for digestion later on back at the office. Learn to recognise them and to respect their right to gather information without undue pressure to engage in conversation. This approach could pay off later, if they decide to approach your company once they've completed their information gathering.

If your stand is really busy, you will need to find a way of concentrating your efforts on people who are there to buy. Work out fairly early into the conversation whether someone is in the market for your product (or will be in the near future) or whether they are simply time-wasters (or even competitors!). Introduce yourself and ask a few questions to help establish whether this person is genuine. Simply ask which company they're from and what their role is, ask for a business card, or look at their name badge. Should you find yourself stuck with a time-waster, get rid of them – politely! 'Let me get a brochure for you, which you can flick through over a cup of coffee. Jamie, can you get Mr Smith a coffee please? It's been lovely chatting. Thank you so much for visiting our stand and I do hope to see you again before too long.' Who could possibly object to a polite brush-off like that?

Staffing your stand: dos and don'ts

- Don't allow anyone on the stand to do more that three hours without a break, as staffing a stand is really hard work. Draw up a rota. An average-sized stand at an all-day exhibition attracting 10,000 people requires three staff, two on duty and one available to relieve staff for their breaks, to free them to visit other stands and to engage in networking.

- Do fully brief staff on what you hope to get out of the event and what is expected of each of them individually as well as collectively. Set targets for how many business cards or leads you want to collect, how many appointments you would like set up, how many demonstrations should be performed and so on.

- Don't let staff huddle in groups on your stand, laughing and chatting to each other rather than customers. Never let them sit down and relax or read at the stand; use the telephone; eat, drink or leave used coffee cups about the place; or leave the stand unattended.

- Do make sure everyone understands how they should handle interest, enquiries and difficulties.

- Don't forget that you'll be busy schmoosing customers, so someone else will need to be in charge of keeping an eye on things, checking that the stand is tidy and well stocked and that staff are doing what they're supposed to be doing and remain motivated and active.

- Do remember that the visitor flow will not be consistent: there will be busy times and quiet periods. Staff your stand accordingly. Make sure plenty of people are around at peak times, such as when talks or seminars end, and in the mid-morning and mid-afternoon periods. Let them take their breaks during the lulls.

- Don't overstaff your stand, as this leaves visitors reluctant to approach for fear of being pounced on and sold to. Don't allow staff to hover, ready to swoop on unsuspecting passers-by. Instead, get them to adopt an encouraging stance at the stand.

Capturing enquiries and following up on leads

Set up a system in advance so that you can record the details of people who buy, people who show a strong interest, and those you promised to get in touch with afterwards. Capturing leads is key to sales success. They're your future customers – but only if you follow up with each and every one of them later. To enable you to make a tailored approach after the event, make sure you have their full contact details (just ask for a business card), an idea of where they fit within their company, a note of their interests and needs, budget, likely buying timescale, plus anything else that is useful to you. Write this all down as soon as you have finished talking to them, while it is all fresh in your mind. If you are in the enviable position of generating a large number of leads, try to prioritise them. Make a note of how warm or hot they are, so that you can follow up red-hot leads straight away and eventually get round to the lukewarm ones when the others are dealt with.

Once the big day is over, it's tempting to sit back and relax. Don't! First, hold a post mortem. Discuss what worked and what was not so good. Learn from your mistakes, and learn from other's too. What ideas did you pick up from other exhibitors? How can this knowledge and insight be put to good use next time? Check your achievements against your objectives to evaluate how successful the venture was. Did you make a profit on the day from sales and orders?

'Capturing leads is key to sales success.'

Next follow up with leads and contacts collected during the event. How does the maths look once you've added in sales made subsequently as a result of following up leads? Now was it a worthwhile enterprise overall?

One pleasant side effect of exhibiting can be an upturn in trade immediately after an event. Make sure you have sufficient staff and stock in place to cope with any increased business after a trade show.

Action points

- Assess whether exhibitions could play a part in your sales strategy. Draw up a list of events, exhibitions or trade fairs that might be suitable and request further information about the cost of exhibiting and visitor profiles.

- If you are thinking of exhibiting for the first time, attend one or two events and pick up ideas on how others approach it professionally.

- If you currently routinely exhibit, take a critical look at how you do things. Does your stand and display material pass muster? Is your sales team the best it can be – well briefed, clear on goals, with great interpersonal skills? List areas for improvement then tackle them.

Summing Up

- In this chapter we covered the basics of selling at exhibitions, from how to identify the best showcase for your wares through to how to evaluate whether or not the event was successful.

- Dos and don'ts reminded us of what we should be doing – smiling, listening, chatting, capturing leads and following up afterwards – and what we should avoid.

- Cardinal sins include poor planning beforehand, an unprofessional approach on the day, and half-hearted or non-existent follow up of leads and contacts in the days, weeks and months after the event.

Chapter Six

Simple Ways to Boost Sales

Take a look at your sales figures for the last three years. Have they increased year-on-year? What kinds of things have you done to boost sales? Have you been proactive or are you guilty of sitting back and waiting for growth to happen all by itself? To be effective in sales, you must be on your toes, coming up with creative ideas to increase turnover.

One of the easiest ways to boost sales is to sell benefits rather than features. By simply rewording your offer to major on benefits, you will turn more wavering prospects into fully fledged customers, with all the positive impact that that will have on your bottom line.

Sell features, not benefits

Many small businesses focus on a product's features when they're selling, without realising that customers buy benefits. To sell more, sell benefits. Whether you're selling face-to-face or through an advert or mailshot, flag up the benefits gained by your customers from the features of your product. Not sure of the difference? Well, take a look at the example overleaf for a pair of shoes:

'One of the easiest ways to boost sales is to sell benefits rather than features.'

Shoe's feature	Benefits to customers
Unique rubberised 'Flexite' sole	Lasts longer than ordinary soles, meaning that shoes stay smarter for longer and cost less in repairs
Double-padded uppers	Provides extra comfort, prevents blisters and keeps feet much warmer than standard shoes
Extra under-heel padding	Acts like a shock absorber to cushion the heel, allowing you to walk miles further with less foot fatigue

The average consumer does not go out specifically looking for a rubberised Flexite sole and double-padded uppers, but lots of us would love shoes that were really comfy, guarded against blisters and kept the feet warm in winter. When we shop, we want to know what's in it for us. We don't care too much for the technical specifications of products (with a few exceptions – particularly in the technical B2B market) but we do want to know what kind of benefits we can expect that will make us more comfortable, more beautiful, more healthy, etc.

Here's another example to illustrate the difference between features and benefits. In this one, the virtues of key manufacturing features are extolled at the expense of the more saleable benefits for buyers: 'This Scotchsafe-coated craftsman-built armchair has dovetail joints reinforced with aluminium rivets driven deep into the chair's hardwood sub-frame, giving it a rigid construction'. To focus on benefits, simply reword to: 'This craftsman-built armchair is so strong that it will last for decades. Its tough, invisible protective coating guards against spills and stains, keeping your chair's upholstery fresh as new and dispensing with the need for expensive shampooing and cleaning'.

Even when selling products where technical specifications are important, don't neglect the benefits. Those as old as I am may recall that hilarious Not the Nine O'Clock News sketch in which a man goes into a hi-fi shop and is bamboozled with technical talk about whether or not he wants 'woofers and tweeters' and other technical features. Don't just say that your camera has a Zigot lens; explain how that allows it to take sharp, high quality images. Never allow yourself to become a feature freak.

Competitive quotes

Are you ever asked to quote for a piece of work? What is your success rate? If you are often approached to quote for a job, yet seldom win, it may not be your pricing that's at fault: perhaps it's the way you set out your quotation that's to blame. Take the two following examples for redecorating a room.

P&W Decorators Limited
QUOTATION

Redecoration of dining room   £715 (plus VAT)

NB Wallpaper not included in price

It's not a compelling piece of salespersonship, making the cardinal mistake of failing to recognise that an opportunity to quote is more than just the chance to tell someone how much you will charge for a job. It's a sales opportunity, so grab it and prepare a quote that is a compelling case for the customer to say yes.

The version on the following page, for the same job, is so much better.

Perfection Painting and Decorating

Our mission is to make you happy!

QUOTATION

- Rake out old, crumbling plaster

- Apply plasterboard and two coats of skim

- Strip walls and rub down skirting boards, architrave and door

- Apply quality lining paper to walls

- Paper walls in client's wallpaper

- Apply lining paper to ceiling and paint with two coats of emulsion

- Apply undercoat and two coats of gloss paint to all woodwork

- Clean up afterwards. Bag up, remove and safely dispose of all debris

£785 plus VAT

(With the exception of the top wall covering, this price includes all supplies – undercoat, paint, paste, lining paper, plaster board, plaster etc.)

'Without doubt the best decorating company I have ever used and I cannot commend them highly enough. They went the extra mile – then some!'
Mrs Janet Rhodes, Anytown

Winner of the Anytown Chamber of Commerce Best Customer Service 2012
Member of Society of Quality Decorators

Which would you choose? I'd select Perfection Painting and Decorating and happily pay £70 more. Perhaps both companies will undertake the same work to the same standard, making P&W Decorators the better choice, but why take the risk? The customers knows what they're getting with Perfection Painting because they've gone to the trouble of itemising the offering and have given the impression that lots of extras are thrown in, such as materials and the clean up afterwards. They have also demonstrated their commitment to great customer care, by using a strapline, publicising their customer service award and including a testimonial from a happy customer. Use the quotation as an opportunity to get your prospect excited about the purchase rather than depressed about the cost.

Incentivising customers

Another great way to boost sales is to offer incentives. People love to get something for nothing. A wedding dress shop that offers free alterations will get more business that one that charges, even though the overall cost may be the same. A £500 dress with free alterations will 'feel' better value than an identical dress priced up at £450 with a £50 charge for alterations. Be careful how you word your incentive. Anything that is given away 'free' will, in reality, be incorporated into your pricing structure. State that alterations are included in the price, and those not requiring the service may feel short-changed, while customers needing alterations will know that they are paying for it. No one will feel they've got a good deal. By offering it free, you please everyone and your incentive should help boost sales.

'Use the quotation as an opportunity to get your prospect excited about the purchase rather than depressed about the cost.'

Use incentives to persuade customers to:

- Buy from you rather than a competitor – My local café offers a free chocolate with every hot drink. It costs them next to nothing but it's sufficient to persuade me, a hardened chocoholic, to go there rather than to the otherwise similar café over the road.

- Switch from a competitor – If a customer feels no loyalty towards their current supplier, even a small incentive may be enough to tip the balance in your favour and get them to switch their business.

- Buy without delay – Consider offering customers a small free gift or other incentive (such as free delivery), but only if they place an order before a certain deadline. This is an effective way of prodding customers into action; left to their own devices, they may not otherwise get round to ordering.

- Buy during quiet periods – An incentive can help generate much-needed trade during slack periods. Restaurants typically have to turn away trade during the busy December run-up to Christmas, yet often find their tables empty in January.

- Buy more of your product – By offering an incentive for sales over a certain value or number of units, you may encourage customers to buy more than they might otherwise. Simply offering mail order customers free postage on orders over £40 might be sufficient to persuade some to increase the total value of their purchases to qualify for the incentive.

- Try a new product – Many of us dislike change and tend to stick with the tried and tested. An incentive might be required to persuade your customers to try your new, possibly more expensive range.

When considering incentives, think carefully about what inducement you would offer and whether it would be likely to boost sales by enough to not only cover its costs but to show you an improvement in your sales figures. Keep a close eye on your sales statistics to check that any incentive is paying its way. To measure the effectiveness of an incentive on sales, offer it to one group of customers but not to another similar group. Measure take-up and see if the incentivised group was significantly more responsive than the control group.

'Keep a close eye on your sales statistics to check that any incentive is paying its way.'

Incentive dos and don'ts

- Do ensure that your chosen incentive will be valued by your customer, however small it may be.

- Don't offer shoddy, nasty or tacky incentives that will create a negative image of your business.

- Do offer an appropriate incentive. A free paintbrush might be a great deal-clincher when selling paint, but be of no interest to customers buying baked beans.

- Don't forget that an incentive may help you to win back lost customers. Consider sending lapsed customers a special money-off voucher or some other inducement to place an order. Make them really feel like you value their custom and have missed them.

Customer incentive, reward or loyalty programmes

Reward programmes can be as simple as the cards many coffee shops provide to customers. The card is stamped each time a purchase is made; after a certain number of stamps have been collected, customers are rewarded with a free hot drink. These simple programmes cost little to set up and run, yet can result in repeat custom and thus sustained sales. It is an easy way to get customers to return to your café rather than to a rival's. Some businesses make loyalty rewards incremental, so that after a certain amount of expenditure or a certain number of visits, the reward increases, with several tiers of reward available – bronze, silver and gold, for example, with corresponding benefits according to the level.

Aside from loyalty schemes, there are other ways of rewarding customer loyalty. Consider writing to your best customers to thank them for their custom; make sure key customers receive a Christmas card; show your appreciation with an occasional money-off coupon or exclusive offer; or invite your best customers to a special dinner or other enjoyable social or corporate event.

Loyalty schemes are worthwhile, as it costs several times more to find a new customer than to hold on to an existing one. Figures quoted vary, but it is generally agreed that it costs several times more to find new customers than to retain them. By that measure, customer reward or loyalty programmes can pay for themselves. However, they are only relevant for businesses where customers make frequent purchasers and can accumulate rewards over a reasonable timescale.

Asking for referrals

Sometimes a business's services are used so infrequently that a loyalty programme would not be worthwhile. For example, you might only use a car showroom every three or four years, or visit your accountant only for your annual tax return. In such businesses, it is difficult to build a meaningful loyalty programme, but incentives still have their place in boosting sales. Aside from knowing your customers' shopping patterns and timing incentives to coincide with their next purchase to ensure they come back to you, you can also incentivise them to recommend friends and family. Give them a reward every time one of their recommended friends makes a purchase. In this way, your customers can become part of your sales team!

Wording your incentive

Sometimes you can achieve a higher level of sales simply by rewording your offer. A book club ran a 'two books for the price of one' promotion in the hope of boosting sales. Not surprisingly the campaign was a success. A short time later it repeated the offer, but this time promoted a 'buy one, get one free' (BOGOF) message. This same deal was far more effective than the previous one. Their customers seemed to prefer the idea of getting one free over a two-for-one promotion. Other research has shown that a BOGOF is more effective than a half-price offer. All of them amount to the same thing, but clearly some are more appealing than others.

But how do you know which offer to offer? Do a test mailing! Use direct mail to systematically change various elements of your offer, and monitor the responses to test the effectiveness of different approaches. Do you get a better response with BOGOF than with a half-price offer? Use a test mailing to find out. Consider running several test mailings simultaneously, perhaps testing half-price, BOGOF and two-for-the-price-of-one offers to see which work best for you.

90

Words that sell

Certain words are tremendously powerful in the sales arena, which is why you see them so often in ads, on product packaging and in sales mailshots. According to research, these attention-grabbing words are: 'new', 'free', 'advice', 'save', 'money', 'reduced', 'how to', 'announcing', 'sex', 'discovery', 'now', 'at last', 'proven', and 'you'. Take a look at them in action below:

'New! Free Advice on How You can Save Money!'

You cannot boost sales simply by stringing a few of them together. If only! But their appropriate use can have an impact, so look out for opportunities to use them in your sales materials, from small newspaper ads and in-store materials, to customer newsletters and other mailings.

Endorsements and testimonials

One of the most powerful ways to sell is by personal recommendation, because people trust others like themselves over salespeople. After all, a salesperson will always have a vested interest in making the sale, whereas a friend or family member will have your best interests at heart. Unfortunately a salesperson will not have a customer's friends permanently on standby to secure the sale, so you will need to rely on endorsements and testimonials to do the job for you.

Endorsements and testimonials lend credibility to your sales claims by reassuring would-be customers that your product assertions are true and can be trusted. You can use the testimonials of ordinary people, you can use celebrity endorsement (although this is generally beyond the means of most small businesses) or you can use a group endorsement, such as describing your camera lens cleaner as the one professional photographers prefer. Such independent, third-party endorsement can give buyers confidence in the quality of the product and therefore remove a possible barrier to them making a purchase.

Do you have letters from customers containing nice comments about your service or products which you can then use as testimonials? No? Then speak to a few customers you know to be satisfied and ask if they will provide a testimonial. You might want to give them a steer on the sort of thing you are

'Endorsements and testimonials lend credibility to your sales claims by reassuring would-be customers that your product assertions are true and can be trusted.'

looking for, but let customers use their own words. Don't worry that they may not phrase it very elegantly or may make grammatical errors: this all lends credibility to the testimonial. Any testimonials you use must be genuine. If possible, seek permission to use the name of the person making it, and perhaps even their photograph. It helps make your testimonial really believable. Testimonials with a handwritten appearance (even in printed publicity) add authenticity too.

Let your vehicles sell for you

Use the name of your company to sell more, without having to resort to expensive advertising. If you are called the Anytown Plumbing Company, residents of Anytown in need of a plumber will know who to contact from having seen your name on vans in the vicinity. An equally good plumber, A&T Limited, will not get that business even though their vehicles are just as visible, because no one will know that they too are a plumbing company serving Anytown. Their name will not spring to mind when a pipe springs a leak! Even if you are not in a position to change the name of your business to make it self-explanatory, you can at least ensure that any company vehicles bear a strapline explaining what you do: 'A&T Limited, Anytown's Premiere Plumbing Company'.

'Cross-selling is the process of selling additional products or services to existing customers.'

Cross-selling

Cross-selling is the process of selling additional products or services to existing customers. For example, a customer might call in to your garage for an MOT and leave – if you are a successful cross-seller – with a freshly valeted car and a set of snow tyres. The benefits for the customer are clear. They are given the opportunity to purchase products that are relevant to them, in one simple visit to a single supplier. For you too, cross-selling is a chance to sell more to each existing customer, thereby boosting your business's profits. The more a customer buys from you, the greater the hassle for them to switch to another supplier. Sell more to each customer and you might hang on to them for longer, all things being equal. However, there are risks. Be careful not to be pushy about trying to sell add-ons or you might end up losing customers. We've all experienced that hard sell at electrical appliance warehouses, where the sales staff try to pressure us into buying overpriced or unnecessary insurance or accessories. This approach can be counterproductive. Effective cross-selling adds value for the customer. For example, a fitted kitchen showroom might, as an add-on, offer (for a price) delivery, installation and removal of the old units. This is something the customer would have had to arrange in any case, and it is more convenient to them to sort out the whole process from the same supplier.

Many businesses miss a trick by neglecting cross-selling. It need not be difficult or hard sell. Sometimes you just have to ask a customer a simple question or tell them about your full product range, then leave it to them to decide whether or not it's of interest.

'I see you're buying some inkjet paper today. Did you know that our inkjet refill cartridges are on special offer until the end of the week? If you buy now, you can save 25 percent.'

'Here's your coffee, sir. Can I get you anything to go with it? We've got some home-made marmalade cake made with organic oranges, or we have delicious scones straight from the oven.'

Cross-selling dos and don'ts

- Do cross-sell only the items that are likely to be of genuine interest to customers.

- Don't be pushy or make the customer feel uncomfortable.

- Do try to tailor the cross-selling opportunity to the customer. A customer buying an umbrella probably won't want to buy special suede cleaner, whereas someone buying suede shoes or a suede bag may find it useful to be told about it.

- Don't be shy about asking, so long as you make it easy for people who are not interested to say no without feeling under pressure or obligation.

Put all of the techniques outlined in this chapter into practice and start reaping the rewards in the form of boosted sales figures.

Action points

- Review your sales literature to check that it promotes benefits over features. If necessary, rewrite it. Do the same with your sales presentation materials.

- Think about how you might be able to introduce a customer loyalty programme aimed at retaining your existing customers or rewarding your best customers, or a referral scheme to attract new customers to your business.

- Do you have slack periods in your business and, if so, could incentives help boost sales during these lean times? Draw up a fully costed programme to make use of incentives with the aim of attracting an upsurge in business during your quiet periods.

Summing Up

- This chapter highlighted some really simple ways of boosting sales, beginning with the importance of reviewing the sales message to check that benefits are being highlighted rather than boring product/service features. People don't want to know that the die-cutting tool's precision plates allow it to cut and emboss; they want to know that they can use it to create fantastic cards and gifts to a professional standard at a fraction of the cost of similar cards in the shops.

- We also examined the use of incentives to increase sales by encouraging customers to stick with you, to switch from rivals, or to buy more of your product than they had planned to.

- We looked at the value of loyalty programmes, especially in light of the high cost of attracting new customers, and the use of endorsements and testimonials in building trust and removing barriers to sales.

- Finally we showed how cross-selling can provide a ready way to boost the bottom line.

Chapter Seven

Setting the Right Price for Profitable Sales

What part does price play in successful selling? If you have a sales role, you are probably already familiar with the 'four Ps' of the marketing mix – product (the thing you sell, which may in fact be a service); place (or distribution – getting your product to buyers); promotion (advertising and so on) and price. To sell successfully, consideration needs to be given to all four – having the right product in the right place, properly promoted so customers know about it and at the right price to ensure profitable sales.

How important is price in your marketing mix? Are your customers very price-conscious, or do other factors matter to them more than the cost of the product? To be successful in sales, you must know the answer to that question. If price is less important than, say, after-sales support or specialist knowledge and expertise, you will be unsuccessful in selling if you focus on price and neglect the things that matter most to the customer. You also risk eroding your profit margin by charging less than you could potentially charge, in the false belief that price is your buyers' overriding concern.

How do you determine prices in your business? Worryingly, quite a few businesses simply pluck a figure from the air that feels about right, and that's what they charge. Some fail to realise (until it is too late) that their chosen prices are too low. This strategy is a sure-fire way to work all hours for little return, and you may even go out of business! Others take an equally simplistic approach. They work out the costs of production, overheads and so on, add in a mark-up (their profit) and hey presto, they've arrived at a price. This approach, too, is no way to run a profitable enterprise. Many salespeople fail to realise that they may be able to charge a lot more for their goods and therefore make a lot more profit for no extra effort. Price-setting is an essential activity for

'Are your customers very price-conscious, or do other factors matter to them more than the cost of the product? To be successful in sales, you must know the answer to that question.'

any business, the aim being to reach the optimum price: one that is profitable for you, and that the market will accept. A vital component of this process is that of monitoring the competition.

- What do competitors charge? Make sure that you know what the going rate is for your service or product.
- What is included in the price your rivals charge? Research competitors and try to understand their pricing structure.
- What do you do/offer/include that differentiates you from competitors?
- What kind of a premium does that unique difference add to the value of your offering?

You might find that a rival consultant charges £50 per hour for their services. Should you charge a bit less so that you're seen to be more competitive in order to boost your client list? Or a bit more, because you're more experienced than her? Or perhaps you should charge two, three, even four times as much? There's no simple formula for price-setting that guarantees sales. It all depends. You can charge much, much more if you can demonstrate the value of your service to customers, over the value of your rivals' offerings. Let's say that a day of one of your competitor consultant's time leads, on average, to savings for companies of £1,000 per annum. An investment of £350 a day for that advice seems like a fair deal. But no company would want to employ you for £1,000 per hour if your advice saved them a similar amount. However, if you could prove that an outlay of £7,000 for a day of your time could produce savings of over £100,000 per annum, your hourly rate would seem cheap in comparison! So to sell your offering at a higher price, you need to be able to show in a tangible way that your price is worth every penny. Remember that you're not selling your time at £150 per hour; you're selling your 25 years of experience. It took you a quarter of a century to gain it, but you're willing to share it for just £150 an hour. What a bargain!

How to charge more

In a price-sensitive market, a business ignores price at its peril. But not all markets are price-conscious, and you may find that you can boost your bottom line simply by charging more – and getting away with it. When I first set up as a consultant, my hourly rate was set too low, at around half of what similarly-experienced consultants were charging. Despite my low fees, I couldn't understand why they were picking up more contracts than me. It took me a while to find the answer: people felt that with such low fees, I mustn't be any good! I put up my rates and my client list really took off. Many people believe that you get what you pay for and equate low prices with cheap, shoddy products and slapdash service. Conversely, they perceive more expensive products to be higher quality, even if in reality they are identical to their cheaper rivals. So don't automatically assume that low prices will result in high sales; all too often they merely result in low profits!

Never under-price

Research shows time and again that most of us find it impossible to distinguish cheaper from more expensive products in 'blind' tests. That's why discount supermarkets' products often rank higher than premium brands in blind taste tests. However, if you 'accidentally' let your tasters catch sight of prices during the blind test, they are likely to claim to prefer the pricier product – even when the researchers have mischievously swapped price tags so that the expensive product bears a cheap label and vice versa! In one test, three samples of whisky – a cheap, a medium-priced and an expensive – were offered to tasters. The higher the price, the higher the perceived quality. The researchers had sneakily given out the same whisky for all three samples!

Price is usually a factor, but it's rarely the only one. Reliability, trustworthiness, reputation, knowledge and expertise, styling, product range, credit terms, speed of delivery, a better guarantee, more flexibility, better after-sales or technical support, convenience, friendliness, exclusivity . . . there are so many other factors that will persuade someone to buy from you – even when you are a bit more expensive than your competitors. To charge more than rival businesses, you'll need to have something extra, an edge, that gives you a much higher perceived value among your customers that justifies the extra cost to them. Spell it out so that customers can see the value.

My husband gets his hair done at a local barber shop for a very reasonable price. His friend goes to an expensive salon in town and pays three times as much for a similar cut. Why? Because they give him a cold beer and an iPad to play with while he's waiting, and a relaxing head massage during his wash. He just loves it! This small additional outlay by the hairdresser allows them to reap

'Don't automatically assume that low prices will result in high sales; all too often they merely result in low profits!'

big rewards when it comes to pricing their service, and their customers are happy to pay for it. How can you add value to your product without adding too much extra cost? A gift shop near me will gift-wrap purchases free of charge and is always packed with customers in the lead up to Mother's Day, Valentine's Day and at other peak gift-buying periods.

Quantify the value

It's one thing to charge a slightly higher price, but if your prices are significantly above those of others, some explanation may be required. It is not uncommon in service industries, particularly consultancy, for prices to vary quite widely and potential customers can find it hard to compare prices when they may not be comparing like with like. What makes your design consultancy better than the one down the road that charges half as much? It's a question that customers will want answered. Replying that you're better than your rivals is insufficient. Quantify it. Help customers to understand how a relationship with you will be more like an investment than an expenditure. Make this tangible. Show how you will boost their profitability or improve their effectiveness. Demonstrate the return they will get from their initial outlay. Help them to understand the value of doing business with you.

'Help customers to understand how a relationship with you will be more like an investment than an expenditure.'

The perceived value of your product or service is not fixed. You can influence it through effective branding. By positioning your product as an exclusive or luxury item, with corresponding luxe packaging and all the other feel-good trimmings, people who want a special treat or who see themselves as a cut above, may be willing to pay significantly more for it. Luxury, gift-wrapped soap with an exotic name, wonderful fragrance, fancy box and exuberant ribbon may cost 20 percent more to manufacture than household toilet soap, yet sell for ten or more times as much. This works for services too. People expect to pay more for services delivered in plush surroundings. Can you reposition your product or service so that it is high-end, with a correspondingly higher-end price tag?

Supply and demand also affects price and if demand is high but supply is limited, prices can rise. Say you get your hands on a container load of genuine 1970s' flared trousers in psychedelic colours just as vintage flares come back into fashion, you'll be able to name your price. In trendy parts of London people might happily part with £200 for a pair. But the minute vintage flares fall out of fashion, you'll struggle to offload your stock at even rock-bottom prices. If supply of your product or service is limited, consider upping your prices and so long as there is good demand, you will make a great profit.

Pricing convenience

Another way to charge more for the same is to put a price on convenience. A plumber who visits your home during the day, to a booked appointment, will charge less the same plumber who is roused from his bed at midnight to an urgent call-out. The customer could wait until morning to call him, but recognises that a premium price for an emergency plumbing service is cheaper than a flooded house and the total destruction of treasured belongings. Think about how you can structure your offering so that there are times when you can up your prices in return for delivering faster, providing a guaranteed delivery date, working over the weekend to get a job finished or offering some other facility that is beyond the norm and valued by customers.

Customers may not be price-conscious

Sometimes our customers are less price-conscious than we realise. Do you know for sure that price is a key factor for them? How do you know? For customers buying your product or service for the first time, or making a one-off purchase, they may have no price reference point. If they have never used a lawyer before to draw up a contract of employment or to do their conveyancing, how do they know what the going rate is? They probably don't. That's not an invitation to rip them off, but it's a useful reminder that not all of your customers or clients will necessarily buy on price alone. Think about your own customers and the importance of price to them. Organise some focus groups or undertake other research to fully understand where price fits into the decision-making process for your customers. Is it a top priority, or does it languish near the bottom of their list?

One way to set prices that are on the high side, without your clients ever realising, is to price up for the job rather than by the hour. Rather than saying that your rate is £100 per hour, say that it will cost £100 to fix the faulty car (or better still, round it down to £99). This stops customers from comparing your hourly rate with their own, and gets them thinking instead that £99 is a fair price to get their car back on the road. Be careful with your calculations, as you don't want to find that a job you thought would take two hours ends up taking the whole day, but you've already agreed a fixed fee for the job and end up out of pocket.

You might find that you can boost sales revenues simply by a small price increase without anyone even noticing. If you need a bigger price increase, one that will not go unnoticed, use it to your advantage and turn the bad news into good news. Warn your most loyal customers of the impending increase and invite them to stock up at the old price. It's a clever way of boosting sales and making your best customers feel they are getting an exclusive bargain.

Creativity in discounting

'Failure to monitor market prices may make selling hard, impossible even, in a price–sensitive market.'

The ideal scenario is the one discussed previously, where higher prices lead to more (and sustained) purchases by happy customers. Regrettably there are times when even our normal prices, let alone higher ones, are too much and we need to drop prices to boost sales. For those operating in a very price-conscious environment, price-monitoring of competitors is key, because you can be sure that customers will be doing that too, constantly comparing prices in order to secure the best deal. Should a rival company drop prices, you will need to consider your position. Failure to monitor market prices may make selling hard, impossible even, in a price-sensitive market. Equally, a knee-jerk price drop in response to a rival's discounts may leave you selling at a loss. No business can survive for long when trading in this way – including your knock-down price competitors, so never panic when they price-drop. They cannot sustain it in the longer term.

You may need to discount for a variety of reasons, not necessarily related to competitor activity. It may be that you have entered a slack period (such as traditionally the time after Christmas when customers are broke), or that you have excess stock that needs to be shifted, or poor-selling lines that must be cleared out to make space for new product ranges. When discounting, never just drop prices; try to be a bit more creative than that and make sure that there's something in the deal for you too.

Discounting dos and don'ts

■ Don't offer an open-ended 25 percent off: combine it with a time limit so customers feel that they must hurry to take advantage of your special price. This will allow you to shift products quickly.

■ Do use a discount as a means of bumping up the size of orders. Offer the discount only if the value of the order exceeds a certain amount, or only if the customer buys at least two of them, or at least one full-price item as well.

■ Don't automatically offer a discount to all customers. Consider making some discounts exclusive to your best customers, so that they feel valued. Their reward is an exclusive reduction; yours is a customer who is more likely to remain loyal.

■ Do consider using a free gift as an alternative to a discount. A gift with a high perceived value to the customer may actually cost you very little – less than any cash discount you may have been contemplating.

■ Don't discount as a knee-jerk response to falling sales. Investigate the cause and tackle that first. You may find that if you improve your customer care or tackle other shortcomings, there will be no need to discount to attract sales.

■ Do consider building a permanent discount into your pricing structure to boost demand during slack periods. A beauty salon that is always quiet on a Monday might run half-price offers on that day to help recoup some fixed costs. Everyone gains. You help cover your fixed costs, your customers benefit from a discount, and you free up capacity by dealing with customers on quiet days rather than on your busiest ones.

■ Don't necessarily offer the discount now. Promise that orders placed this month at the normal price will earn customers a guaranteed reduction off any orders placed next month. At least that way you will get some repeat business.

One way to discount to your advantage is to offer differential pricing. Your high rate can be charged for clients who want a job done now, whereas a client who is willing to let you slot their job in at your convenience can get a discount. The benefit is that you are under no pressure to get their reduced price job done straight away, saving you the stress of deadlines and the pain of having to work evenings and weekends to get it finished on time.

Remember that ultimately, there's more to life that making the sale so don't secure it at any cost. Never price a job so low that you or your colleagues end up feeling resentful about undertaking a job with such a poor return for all that hard work. Eager though you will be to make a sale, sometimes you just have to accept that it's best to walk away. There will be other opportunities in the future.

Loss leaders

Another creative way to discount is to offer 'loss leaders', products (or services) that are sold at, or even below, cost price, usually for a limited period, as a way to attract customers, who will then buy other products and give you an overall net profit on their transactions. It's best to offer as loss leaders products whose price is well known to customers, so they know at a glance that your special offer is really terrific. When using this strategy, be sure that customers will buy more than just your loss leader items (you don't want to bankrupt yourself!). You could offer a half-price manicure, but only if the customer buys two premium nail varnishes. Also be careful that customers don't stockpile – perhaps by limiting the number they can buy, limiting the amount of stock that will be available at that price, or limiting these offers to perishable items that cannot be stockpiled. Keep a close eye on sales to see whether customers buying your loss leader also bought other goods.

Even consultants and service companies can use the loss leader concept. Whenever I enter the occasional quiet period, I offer key organisations locally a free training workshop that really showcases my ability as a marketing trainer. I have nothing else on, so I'm not losing income, and it's a great way to bag new contracts. Companies that would probably say no to paying for a workshop are usually willing to accept one for gratis. Once I've proved my worth to them, they are more receptive to an approach at a later date for paid work, and they always think of me first when they're looking for a marketing trainer.

Rounding down

Most businesses price goods at a rounded down price: £9.99 rather than the more logical £10, or £39.95 rather than £40. Knocking off a nominal penny, or 5p, can lead to more sales by making your prices look lower than they really are. £999 feels more than a pound cheaper than the four-digit £1,000 price tag, even though we are perfectly capable of doing the maths. Use psychology and make your prices appear more affordable without having to offer a significant discount.

However, when offering reductions, go for a higher figure. If you are offering discounts of between 30% and 70%, 'Up to 70% off' is better than 'Discounts from 30% upwards.'

Action points

▩ Are there times when you can charge a higher price? People are willing to pay more for first class post, peak rate travel and high season holidays. Examine the potential in your business for differential pricing.

▩ What are the factors that are important to your customers when buying from you? Is it price, something else, or a combination of factors? Organise some focus group research with customers so that you really understand where price fits in your marketing mix.

▩ Consider whether you can make use of loss leaders to boost sales.

'Use psychology and make your prices appear more affordable without having to offer a significant discount.'

Summing Up

- In this chapter we examined the importance of price in your business's marketing strategy.

- We looked at price-sensitive markets and how to discount creatively – from loss leaders to deferred discounts.

- We also studied the importance of not focusing solely on price, including opportunities to charge more by adding value without adding cost.

- Finally, our whistle-stop tour of the subject concluded with a brief nod at the psychology of prices and discounts, including the need to round prices down and home in on the highest discount.

Chapter Eight

Great Customer Service Boosts Sales

Treat customers badly and they will walk; treat them well and they will be loyal. You don't need a book to tell you that. Why, then, do so many companies – from small, local businesses to big household names – provide such shoddy customer service, when it is self-evident that it can do nothing but damage their business?

Recently I called into a bank to open an account for my teenage daughter. At a time when banks are struggling to be profitable, you think they'd welcome a new customer. Their response: 'Can you call back on another day, as we're really busy today.' I cast my eyes in disbelief around the empty banking hall. I won't bore you with the rest of the interaction, but suffice it to say that my daughter decided that this was not the bank for her. The bank's marketing was great. It did its job in attracting us in to open an account, but abysmal customer service let it down and now they've lost a customer. Poor customer service = lost sales – now and in the future. That bank will never get the benefit of the high salary I hope my daughter will go on to earn. It will never get the profits from the big mortgage that she will go on to take out. It will not get her buildings and contents insurance, her pension, her investments. All the cashier saw was a spotty teenager presenting herself on a Saturday afternoon when no one could be bothered to open an account for her. Yet she will go on to have a very profitable lifetime value for one lucky bank.

So, perhaps it's not so obvious that customer care is important, when big companies like that can get it so badly wrong. Small ones too. Think about the last time you asked tradesmen to call at your home or workplace to provide estimates. How many of them turned up at all, let alone on time? Good service does exist, but poor service is all too widespread.

As a salesperson, you know it makes sense to get your customer service right, but here's a cogent reminder of why:

- It is cheaper to keep an existing customer than to attract a new one. While there is no agreed figure on the costs involved, it is said that it can cost between three and 30 times as much to win a new customer as to keep an old one.

- Happy customers make repeat purchases and boost your sales figures by recommending you to their friends and family; unhappy customers take their custom elsewhere and encourage their contacts to do likewise, which will have an adverse impact on your sales figures.

- Good customer service can differentiate your business from competitors offering otherwise similar goods or services, tipping the balance in your favour and boosting sales.

- Good customer service enhances your reputation and makes it easier for you to sell to new customers; bad customer care damages reputation and potential customers may be unwilling to chance doing business with you.

It's pretty obvious, then, that treating customers well makes financial sense, but have you ever stopped to consider quite how much financial sense it makes?

Calculating a customer's lifetime value

When a business loses a customer through poor customer service, it's easy to shrug the shoulders. After all, it's just one customer among many, and they only spend £30 a time with you. Will you really miss such a paltry sum? This is short-sighted, because every customer is valuable and, looked at over their lifetime, they may be more valuable than you realise. Here's how to calculate the value of each customer to your business.

Work out the value of your average sale (annual sales in £s ÷ number of transactions).	A = £
Estimate (or, if you have the data, use actual figures) the average number of purchases annually from each regular customer.	B=

Multiply B by the average number of years that a customer remains active	C =
How many referrals/recommendations do your existing customers make?	D =

Using those figures, work out the sums below:

The annual value of your average customer: A .... x B .... = F £................

The lifetime value of your average customer: F .... x C .... = G £................

The value of gross sales from referrals   G .... x D .... = I £.................

Ta da! Now calculate the total lifetime value of a satisfied customer

G ....+ I .... = £ ....

Here's how it works in practice. Let's say that you run a garage:

Your average sale is £150 (A)

Each regular customer visits you twice a year, once for an MOT and once for a service (B)

Your customers stick with you for around 7 years (C)

Each recommends two of their friends to you (D).

Here's how you work out the value of one customer:

Sales per customer per year = A x B (i.e. £150 x 2) = £300 (F)

Sales per customer over a lifetime = F x C (i.e. £300 x 7) = £2,100 (G)

Gross sales from referrals = G x D (i.e. £2100 x 2) = £4,200 (I)

Total value of a satisfied customer = G + I (i.e. £2,100 + £4,200) = £6,300

Work out the lifetime value of your customers, then next time you feel irritated with a customer and feel like telling them to take a running jump, take a deep breath instead, smile sweetly, and remind yourself that they're worth thousands to your business!

Systematising great customer service

Do you provide excellent customer service? Do you always get it right before, during and after the sale? When potential customers make an enquiry, do you respond enthusiastically and supply information or a quotation in an appropriate timescale? Do you remember to send out the literature they requested or to phone and check that they have everything they need? Do you follow up after each sale to check that all is well? Are all of your sales and front-line staff friendly and helpful? Do they smile and welcome visitors or shoppers? Do they answer the telephone quickly and deal with calls courteously and efficiently? Is there a clear system for offering visitors a cup of coffee, or is it left to chance?

Great customer service is never a chance thing; it is a planned series of activities designed to ensure that a customer is left satisfied after any interaction with your business. It's an important area because it directly affects the bottom line of your business. Your sales role will be impossible if your company has a lousy reputation and the only links a search engine generates are those to websites that criticise your service and your products. How can you possibly make sales in that kind of environment?

Brilliant customer service – getting it right and then going a bit further than expected – need not cost anything at all, but it can make you serious money if you know how to do it. Take my hairdresser, a busy provincial salon. I pay over the odds to go there because I like the things that they get right: small, but important things. They remember that I take my coffee black with no sugar and that I like their mango hair conditioner; they text my phone to remind me of my impending hair appointment; they serve a complimentary glass of wine to Friday-evening customers to get them in the mood for a night out; they give clients a mince pie at Christmas and send them a Christmas card with a £10 hairdressing gift voucher to use in January . . . These little things make me feel more than just one of many customers: they make me feel valued.

Is my hairdresser a wonderful, caring person who remembers each and every customer? No, she's just a great salesperson, because she has recognised the value of great customer care as a means of hanging on to existing customers and expanding her customer base through recommendation. She doesn't really remember how I like my coffee, but she makes the effort to record these kinds of details on her computer system so that each of her very

'Great customer service is never a chance thing; it is a planned series of activities designed to ensure that a customer is left satisfied after any interaction with your business.'

many customers gets to feel that they are treated as an individual, regardless of which member of her team cuts their hair. She doesn't send me a gift voucher because I'm her friend, but because she knows it makes business sense to cover her overheads by getting me back at her salon during the quiet month of January.

Creating great customer impressions

Work out what you can do to create a great customer impression of your business. Just one bad encounter with one member of staff may reflect on the whole business, undermining your hard work, so create systems to ensure that your vision of perfect customer service is delivered every day, every time, by all of your staff. You might want to specify that certain things must happen at certain times, such as:

- Café tables to be wiped down every 30 minutes.

- Forecourt to be swept at 9am and again at 1pm.

- Fresh flowers to be placed on the reception desk every Monday.

- Window displays to be changed every two weeks.

- Customer toilets to be cleaned on the hour.

- Magazines in the waiting room to be replaced at the end of each month.

- Cushions to be plumped every hour.

- Every customer to be greeted on arrival and offered a hot drink and biscuit.

- 85 percent of orders to be processed and despatched within 24 hours of receipt.

Create a checklist for your business and ensure that each task is assigned to a named individual, who is personally responsible for ensuring that it gets done. Some companies have a simplistic approach to monitoring their customer service performance; they simply count the number of compliments and the number of complaints and use the figures as a gauge of customer satisfaction. The above system of demanding yet achievable customer service standards is better because it sets a standard that can be measured; one that is more reflective of the wider customer experience. Ensure that staff understand the performance level you expect from them and make sure that you (or someone) monitors compliance to ensure consistent quality across all aspects of your company.

Shaping the customer experience

Many different components of your business shape the overall experience for your customers and dictate whether it is good or bad:

▓ Your premises – What image does your reception area or your retail outlet convey about your company? What about the toilets and any other customer facilities? Look at them with fresh eyes and assess whether they are up to scratch. Put right anything that fails to meet the grade.

▓ Your switchboard – How quickly are calls answered? Are callers put through to the right person first time? Are messages taken down accurately and passed on in a timely fashion? Set a standard so staff know how quickly to answer the phone or how promptly to return calls.

▓ Your vehicles – Are they clean and tidy at all times, and driven with courtesy to other road-users? I'm unlikely to want to use a company whose drivers think they're boy racers.

▓ Your admin systems – How quickly do you acknowledge post and emails? How speedy are you in fulfilling orders? Inefficiency and slowness reflect badly, so sharpen up your act and enhance the customer experience.

▓ Your tills – How quickly are customers served? How long are customers kept waiting? Can you speed things up by re-rostering so that peak periods are covered by sufficient staff? Set a standard (such as maximum queuing time, three minutes) and monitor performance to ensure that you are meeting it.

Customer service dos and don'ts

▓ Do ensure that staff know how to respond to adverse comments positively and undefensively.

▓ Don't expect staff to be instinctively good at customer service: train them. New shop staff receive more training in handling money than in handling people, yet unless they handle people properly, they won't be handling much money.

'Don't expect staff to be instinctively good at customer service: train them.'

- Do remember that front-line staff such as receptionists, telephonists and sales assistants are key to quality customer service, as they create the first impressions of any business. Remember to include them in customer service training.

- Don't strip staff of their individuality by over-programming them, forcing them to robotically ask customers if everything was alright, or giving them a turgid script to recite when they answer the phone.

- Do let your staff's (friendly) personality shine through and encourage them to take a genuine interest in the customer's experience – including empowering them to put things right if the company falls short of its usual standards.

Dealing with problems

However good your customer service systems, there will be times when mistakes are made or customers are left unhappy. The way you deal with such situations is crucial, and can make the difference between, at one end of the scale, turning the customer into an ambassador for your company; or at the other end, losing their custom altogether.

Most of us are reluctant to make formal complaints. How often do you complain about poor service? Every time you encounter it? Probably not. (Ninety-six percent of dissatisfied customers do not complain.) But chances are that you do grumble to others about it, and recount your experiences. On average we tell seven others what happened, and some of us go on to tell anyone who'll listen about our bad experiences at the hands of other companies. You can see the full impact of that in the diagram overleaf.

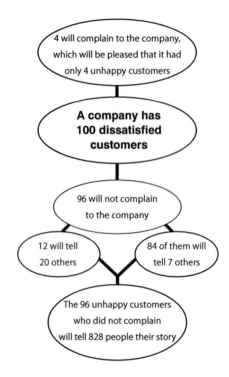

4 will complain to the company, which will be pleased that it had only 4 unhappy customers

A company has 100 dissatisfied customers

96 will not complain to the company

12 will tell 20 others

84 of them will tell 7 others

The 96 unhappy customers who did not complain will tell 828 people their story

Although there are some people who will complain about anything at the drop of a hat, most of those who get round to complaining are seriously unhappy, and often with good reason. Take their complaint seriously and try to retrieve the situation.

To help avert complaints in the first place, conduct routine customer satisfaction surveys and act on the results; give one of your team responsibility for customer care; and respond to feedback on comments and suggestions cards. When someone wants to complain, make it easy for them. Produce an easy-to-complete tick box style complaints card, and set out your official complaints procedure using friendly, plain language and make it available on your website.

Regard dissatisfied customers as satisfied customers in the making, because much research indicates that a dissatisfied customer who is dealt with fairly, promptly and courteously is more likely to be loyal to you than one who has never had cause to complain.

Dos and don'ts of dealing with complaints

- Do always remain calm, polite and helpful, however angry or unreasonable you think the complainer is. Listen and let them make their case. Never interrupt, argue or lose your temper.

- Don't forget that if the matter being complained of was your company's fault, you should always offer a genuine apology and propose corrective action.

- Do remember that where a complaint is serious, it might be helpful to discuss the problem (and resolution) face-to-face rather than through an exchange of correspondence.

- Don't get into a position where complaints letters are to-ing and fro-ing for months on end; you will not get a happy complainer at the end. Try to resolve the matter at the earliest stage.

- Do encourage complaints and always put right any organisational or systems failures that prompted the complaint in the first place.

- Don't just do the minimum. Go beyond that if you can, and where appropriate, offer compensation.

- Do ensure that all staff accept responsibility for the company's failures, regardless of whether the failure was their own or someone else's. It is of no interest to the customer that you are short-staffed or that you work in a different part of the business; as a representative of the company, they hold you responsible. Passing a customer from pillar to post will only add to their dissatisfaction and give them another cause for complaint.

Much poor customer service is low level and stems from a can't-be-bothered-to-help/think attitude. Here are some typical examples:

'Regard dissatisfied customers as satisfied customers in the making.'

Bad customer service	Good customer service
'She's not here. You'll have to ring back.'	'I'm sorry, Sue's out of the office just now. Can I take your details and get her to ring you back this afternoon, or perhaps I can help you myself?'
'Look, it's nothing to do with me. It's not my department. You'll need to speak to the training manager.'	'I'm so sorry to hear that our training department appear to have made a mistake. I can fully understand how frustrating it must be. I'll have a word with the training manager right now and ask her to ring you back within the hour to discuss how we can get this resolved.'
'Be grateful that you've only had to wait three weeks for your delivery! This is our busiest period and you're lucky to have got it that quickly!'	'I am really sorry you've had to wait three weeks. I agree that it's not good enough and I'll personally ensure your order is despatched today. Please accept our apologies for the delay.

Never let such attitudes prevail among your team. Make sure they have a good customer focus.

Create a 'can-do' culture

Many companies have complex and unnecessary rules and regulations that get in the way of good customer service. Staff in these companies adopt a default position that customers' reasonable requests cannot be accommodated. Make sure your staff have a can-do mentality and always do what they can to meet customers' wishes. Pull out all the stops to fulfil a customer's reasonable requests. Never have rules and regulations designed to make life easier for staff, at the expense of customers. Empower staff to be flexible, bending the rules when appropriate in order to keep customers happy. And finally, encourage staff to relish the challenge of unusual or difficult requests, rather than live in fear of them. Do all of this and the results will be clear to see in your sales figures.

Action points

- Sit down with your team and discuss what generally annoys or irritates you when you are a customer. Think of situations where you have received poor customer service. Analyse what went wrong. Draw up an action plan to ensure that your company is never guilty of these things.

- Ask a trusted friend to ring your company with a difficult or awkward question and listen in to see how they are treated. Get someone to write in with a request and note how promptly and efficiently it is handled. This will help you to understand how your customers experience your enterprise. Ask for critical feedback then produce an action plan for tackling shortcomings.

- Test out your rival companies and see how they compare. If you come across any good customer service ideas during this exercise, see if they can be adapted for your own use.

Summing Up

▧ This final chapter examined the value of great customer service in helping to keep existing customers and to attract new ones.

▧ We looked at how to calculate the lifetime value of our average customer and how to systematise customer service to ensure that we keep our customers happy.

▧ We also looked at how to handle unhappy customers and how to turn them into ambassadors for our business.

▧ Finally, we explored the importance of a can-do culture in keeping up customer satisfaction levels.

Help List

Professional Organisations

Chartered Institute of Marketing (CIM)

The Chartered Institute of Marketing
Moor Hall
Cookham
Maidenhead
Berkshire
SL6 9QH
01628 427120
http://www.cim.co.uk
As the world's largest organisation for professional marketers, the CIM offers accredited qualifications and training on marketing issues and has useful information (some chargeable) on sales, branding, market research, pricing, promotions and customer relations on its website. It has branches across the UK.

The Institute of Sales & Marketing Management (ISMM)

The Institute of Sales & Marketing Management
Harrier Court
Lower Woodside
Bedfordshire
LU1 4DQ
Tel: 01582 840001
http://www.ismm.co.uk
The ISMM is the UK's only professional body for salespeople. Founded in 1911 to promote standards of excellence in sales and sales management and to enhance the status and profile of sales as a profession, the ISMM has been the voice of selling and custodian of sales standards, ethics and best practice for over 35 years. Its online resources are accessible to members.

The Marketing Society

The Marketing Society
1 Park Road
Teddington
Middlesex
TW11 0AR
020 8973 1700
http://www.marketing-society.org.uk
This not-for-profit organisation is owned by its members. The Society runs the Marketing Society Awards for Excellence, organises events and talks, publishes various publications and has an online Knowledge Zone with useful resources on sales and a wide range of marketing topics. However, you'll need to be a member to access the Knowledge Zone.

Resources

Business Link

http://www.businesslink.gov.uk
Business Link is the government's online resource for businesses, with easy-to-use tools for small businesses and some really useful plain English resources on topics such as sales and selling, pricing and tendering which can be accessed free of charge.

Federation of Small Businesses

http://www.fsb.org.uk
The Federation of Small Businesses is the UK's largest campaigning pressure group promoting and protecting the interests of the self-employed and owners of small firms. Formed in 1974, it now has 200,000 members across 33 regions and 194 branches and organises training and events, including occasional talks of sales and selling, marketing and regular networking events.

Just Sell Website

http://www.justsell.com/
Lots of practical tips and advice for anyone involved in selling and a free newsletter you can sign up for.

Book List

How to Win Friends and Influence People by Dale Carnegie (Pocket Books)

Although this multi-million bestseller was first published in 1936, it remains a useful and readable book that encourages self-reflection, and understanding of other people and the development of people skills that will make you a better and more confident salesperson.

Essential Managers: Marketing Effectively by Moi Ali (Dorling Kindersley)

In this short, easy-to-use book I look at how to build strong products, develop a brand, achieve growth and create and implement a marketing strategy. All of this provides a useful context for sales and selling.

Need - 2 - Know

Available Titles Include ...

Allergies A Parent's Guide
ISBN 978-1-86144-064-8 £8.99

Autism A Parent's Guide
ISBN 978-1-86144-069-3 £8.99

Blood Pressure The Essential Guide
ISBN 978-1-86144-067-9 £8.99

Dyslexia and Other Learning Difficulties
A Parent's Guide ISBN 978-1-86144-042-6 £8.99

Bullying A Parent's Guide
ISBN 978-1-86144-044-0 £8.99

Epilepsy The Essential Guide
ISBN 978-1-86144-063-1 £8.99

Your First Pregnancy The Essential Guide
ISBN 978-1-86144-066-2 £8.99

Gap Years The Essential Guide
ISBN 978-1-86144-079-2 £8.99

Secondary School A Parent's Guide
ISBN 978-1-86144-093-8 £9.99

Primary School A Parent's Guide
ISBN 978-1-86144-088-4 £9.99

Applying to University The Essential Guide
ISBN 978-1-86144-052-5 £8.99

ADHD The Essential Guide
ISBN 978-1-86144-060-0 £8.99

Student Cookbook – Healthy Eating The Essential Guide
ISBN 978-1-86144-069-3 £8.99

Multiple Sclerosis The Essential Guide
ISBN 978-1-86144-086-0 £8.99

Coeliac Disease The Essential Guide
ISBN 978-1-86144-087-7 £9.99

Special Educational Needs A Parent's Guide
ISBN 978-1-86144-116-4 £9.99

The Pill An Essential Guide
ISBN 978-1-86144-058-7 £8.99

University A Survival Guide
ISBN 978-1-86144-072-3 £8.99

View the full range at **www.need2knowbooks.co.uk**.
To order our titles call **01733 898103**, email **sales@ n2kbooks.com** or visit the website. Selected ebooks available online.

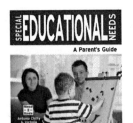

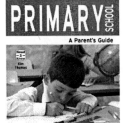
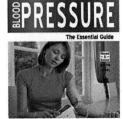
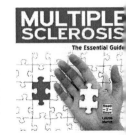

Need - 2 - Know, Remus House, Coltsfoot Drive, Peterborough, PE2 9BF